Teaching Strings in Today's Classroom

Teaching Strings in Today's Classroom: A Guide for Group Instruction assists music education students, in-service teachers, and performers to realize their goals of becoming effective string educators. It introduces readers to the school orchestra environment, presents the foundational concepts needed to teach strings, and provides opportunities for the reader to apply this information. The author describes how becoming an effective string teacher requires three things of equal importance: content knowledge, performance skills, and opportunities to apply the content knowledge and performance skills in a teaching situation.

In two parts, the text addresses the unique context that is teaching strings, a practice with its own objectives and related teaching strategies. Part I (Foundations of Teaching and Learning String Instruments) first presents an overview of the string teaching environment, encouraging the reader to consider how context impacts teaching, followed by practical discussions of instrument sizing and position, chapters on the development of each hand, and instruction for best practices concerning tone production, articulation, and bowing guidelines. Part II (Understanding Fingerings) provides clear guidance for understanding basic finger patterns, positions, and the creation of logical fingerings. String fingerings are abstract and thus difficult to negotiate without years of playing experience—these chapters (and their corresponding interactive online tutorials) distill the content knowledge required to understand string fingerings in a way that non–string players can understand and use.

Teaching Strings in Today's Classroom contains pedagogical information, performance activities, and an online virtual teaching environment with 12 interactive tutorials, three for each of the four string instruments.

Rebecca B. MacLeod is Associate Professor of Music Education at the University of North Carolina at Greensboro (UNCG), where she directs the string education program and conducts the UNCG Sinfonia. She has served on the American String Teachers Association (ASTA) National Board and is past president of the ASTA North Carolina chapter.

Teaching Strings in Today's Classroom

A Guide for Group Instruction

Rebecca B. MacLeod

Routledge
Taylor & Francis Group

NEW YORK AND LONDON

First published 2019
by Routledge
52 Vanderbilt Avenue, New York, NY 10017

and by Routledge
2 Park Square, Milton Park, Abingdon, Oxon, OX14 4RN

Routledge is an imprint of the Taylor & Francis Group, an informa business
© 2019 Taylor & Francis

The right of Rebecca B. MacLeod to be identified as author of this work has been asserted by her in accordance with sections 77 and 78 of the Copyright, Designs and Patents Act 1988.

Library of Congress Cataloging-in-Publication Data
Names: MacLeod, Rachel B., author.
Title: Teaching strings in today's classroom : a guide for group instruction / Rebecca B. MacLeod.
Description: New York ; London : Routledge, 2019. | Includes index.
Identifiers: LCCN 2018035001 (print) | LCCN 2018042212 (ebook) | ISBN 9781351254144 (ebook) | ISBN 9780815368656 (hardback) | ISBN 9780815368670 (pbk.)
Subjects: LCSH: Bowed stringed instruments—Instruction and study.
Classification: LCC MT259 (ebook) | LCC MT259 .M18 2019 (print) | DDC 787/.193071—dc23
LC record available at https://lccn.loc.gov/2018035001

ISBN: 978-0-815-36865-6 (hbk)
ISBN: 978-0-815-36867-0 (pbk)
ISBN: 978-1-351-25414-4 (ebk)

Typeset in Bembo and Helvetica Neue
by Apex CoVantage, LLC

Visit the eResources: www.routledge.com/9780815368670

Contents

Detailed Table of Contents

Preface

The philosophical framework for this textbook is based on the assumption that becoming an effective string teacher requires three things that are of equal importance: (a) content knowledge, (b) performance skills/the ability to model for your students, and (c) the ability to apply the content knowledge and performance skills in a teaching situation. Acquiring performance skills without immediate application in a teaching environment limits an individual's ability to retain the pedagogical information. Mastery of pedagogical information extends beyond an individual's performance ability and includes a deeper understanding of how to both play and teach the instrument. The teacher must be able to assess performance issues and design effective instruction to meet the needs of diverse students with diverse abilities. Actively teaching others while learning to play increases understanding of the instrument because it requires the information to be viewed from multiple perspectives. Focusing only on teaching skills without acquiring a strong pedagogical framework limits the effectiveness of the instructor and thus compromises the abilities of his or her future students. Teaching strings is a unique context with its own objectives and related teaching strategies.

One of the purposes of this book is to provide a resource for the *University String Techniques Course* that addresses these three essential areas: content knowledge, performance activities, and opportunities for direct application as a teacher.

Acknowledgments

This text was inspired by my late mentor, Dr. Michael Allen. He was my role model and inspiration as a string educator. Much of the content in this book is influenced by his teachings. I am forever grateful for the impact that he had on me as a string education and on countless others.

Many people assisted me in the production of this text and I am sincerely thankful. To the students in the Lillian Rauch Beginning Strings Program and Peck Alumni Leadership Program, thank you for agreeing to serve as examples of string instruction in today's classroom. Your passion for music inspires me and I hope it will inspire others to teach. To my students, thank you for providing feedback on the text and tutorials, agreeing to be video recorded and photographed, and for choosing to study with me. To my colleagues Julia Reeves, David Pope, Scott Laird, James Mick, Cody Rex, Bethany Uhler, Julie Ellis, and Brian Carter, your expertise and feedback on the instrument specific chapters was invaluable. Thank you everyone at the University of North Carolina at Greensboro who supported my semester of research leave and provided resources that assisted me in the completion of the text.

The tutorials included in this book were created by Dave Sebald. He spent countless hours coding and revising simply to create something new that may help future teachers. I am indebted to him as a collaborator and hope that we may collaborate again in the future.

Finally, to my husband, Scott MacLeod, and my two beloved dogs, Hope and Domino. Thank you for the hours you allowed me to spend poring over books, taking photos, editing photos, and creating this resource. Without your love and support, I could not have finished.

Rebecca B. MacLeod
May 2018

Videos

Video clips can be accessed on the eResource tab of the book's catalog page: www.rout
ledge.com/9780815368670

Foundations of Teaching and Learning String Instruments

CHAPTER 1

An Introduction to the Orchestra Classroom

WHY TEACH STRINGS?

There are few things more beautiful than watching children receive their first opportunity to play an instrument. Imagine the looks of anticipation, excitement, and joy as students open their cases for the first time. What does the classroom look like in your imagination? What should an effective strings classroom look like? Have you had the opportunity to observe or participate in a heterogeneously grouped string class? How should you structure the first day? What if you have never played a stringed instrument before but are hired to teach orchestra? Where and how should you begin?

Teaching strings is a skill that can be learned and developed by both string players and non-string players alike. In order to become a successful string teacher, one simply needs to understand the fundamental principles of proper setup, tuning, tone production, basic articulations, bowings, fingerings, and instrument maintenance. Once these concepts are mastered, teaching strings becomes logical and intuitive because much of the technique can be assessed visually. Combined with strong musicianship skills, effective sequencing, and classroom management, these foundational principles can guide a teacher through beginning, intermediate, and advanced string instruction in a heterogeneous classroom.

Qualified string teachers are currently in high demand. The number of students who participate in community and school orchestra programs has steadily increased over the last several decades with the support of the National String Project Consortium[1] and El Sistema Programs[2] and through increased participation in public school programs.[3] According to the National String Project Consortium, in 2009 a national shortage of public school string educators was identified with an anticipated need for 3,000 new string teachers. To accommodate the need for string teachers, the number of non-string specialists teaching orchestra has increased over the past two decades.[4,5] Indeed, recent research suggests that nearly one in three string teachers is a non-string player.[6] Preservice teachers frequently question the probability that they may teach outside of their primary content area, or area of interest, but in reality, teaching in multiple areas is increasingly more common. This textbook provides the information needed for interested musicians to become successful and confident string teachers, regardless of their primary musical instrument. String instrument performers will also gain important pedagogical information that will enable them to be successful teaching all four bowed instruments and more effective when communicating about their craft.

Why teach strings?

Because we need more qualified string teachers so that every child has the opportunity to learn.

CULTURALLY RESPONSIVE PEDAGOGY

Cultural background impacts the way in which individuals learn.[7] Characteristics such as language, gender, age, socioeconomic status, religion, and personal beliefs all shape the ways in which people process information. Consider your own experiences growing up. In what type of community did you reside? What language did you speak at home? How did your experiences impact the way that you learned? Many misunderstandings can occur if people are unaware of different societal norms. We make assumptions based on our own experience. For example, if you have always resided in the United States you may be surprised to find that people in the Southern Hemisphere drive north and associate the north with hotter temperatures. Eye contact is culturally specific depending on where you live. Some cultures show respect through eye contact while in others, it may be a sign of disrespect.

The demographics of public school students is becoming increasingly diverse and teachers are expected to increase their cross-cultural competence and global awareness. Teachers who are culturally aware and responsive to their students increase student well-being, motivation, sense of belonging, and achievement.[8] Music, in particular, is connected to culture and identity.[9] For this reason, music teachers should learn as much as possible about students' backgrounds, strengths, and interests. Meeting the needs of every student requires the inclusion of diverse teaching strategies, diverse music, and a student-centered approach that empowers students to share their knowledge with their teacher and peers. String classrooms provide a wonderful opportunity to embrace diversity because string instruments are very eclectic and can be found across a variety of cultures and styles of music.

STRING TEACHING OVERVIEW

String pedagogy is rooted in a strong performance tradition that originated in the private studio. Whereas the public school models for choir and band are based largely on an ensemble approach, performance pedagogues have shaped the field of string education. Individuals such as Ivan Galamian,[10] Kato Havas,[11] William Primrose,[12] Gerhard Mantel,[13] Francois Rabbath,[14] and Franz Simandl[15] contributed approaches commonly used in the private studio. Shinichi Suzuki, Elizabeth Green, and Paul Rolland later provided models for group instruction that transitioned private studio pedagogy into group environments (see boxed information).

Shinichi Suzuki (1898–1998) was a violinist and educator whose teaching centered on the ideal that talent was not inborn but an ability that could be nurtured and taught. He developed the "mother-tongue approach" in which initial music instruction is done through rote activities and imitation, just as a baby learns language. Beginning instruction at an early age (3–4 years), daily music listening, constant repetition, teaching technique through musical literature, and parental involvement are integral aspects of the Suzuki method. https://suzukiassociation.org/about/suzuki-method/shinichi-suzuki/

Elizabeth A. H. Green (1906–1995) impacted the world of string education through her work as a music educator and conducting pedagogue. She taught music education at the University of Michigan while simultaneously teaching high school and middle school orchestra. Her many texts include *Orchestral Bowings and Routines, First Steps in the Galamian Bowing Method, The Modern Conductor, Musicianship and Repertory for the High School Orchestra, Teaching String Instruments in Classes, Increasing the Proficiency on the Violin, The Conductor and his Score, The Dynamic Orchestra*, and *Miraculous Teacher: Ivan Galamian and the Meadowmount Experience*. She is credited with assisting Ivan Galamian in writing *Principles of Violin Playing and Teaching*.

Paul Rolland (1911–1978), originally from Budapest, highly influenced string pedagogy in the United States by focusing on freedom of motion in string playing. His innovative approach, documented in the *Teaching of Action in String Playing*,[16] introduced sequential motions to teach advanced skills such as shifting, vibrato, and off-the-string articulations during the first two years of instruction. He is also one of the founding members of the American String Teachers Association. www.paulrolland.net/index.html

Group string instruction incorporates the philosophies and performance traditions established over centuries of individual instruction. While teaching strings is similar to other group music teaching environments, because of the strong performance traditions that originated with the studio model, a few key differences exist:

1. One of the primary objectives of a beginning string class is proper setup.[17] To achieve this objective, the string teacher must be able to move about the room and assist each student individually. Therefore, the focus on proper setup in the beginning string class influences how the classroom is organized as well as the sequencing and teaching strategies used by the teacher.

2. String specialists model for their students *extensively* during the beginning stages of instruction and avoid conducting the group until the students have developed right-hand skills, left-hand skills, and the ability to read music. During the initial stages of instruction, *all activities are taught by rote.*

3. Developing right-hand skills, left-hand skills, and musicianship skills separately is important to the success of the beginning string student and is recommended by many pedagogues.[18] Most method books written for heterogeneous instruction have adopted this approach. The Suzuki model provides an alternate approach that delays the introduction of music reading and focuses initially on right-hand skills, adding left-hand skills.[19]

4. String teachers manually assist their students to establish the correct bow motion and instrument position. In a public school environment, physically assisting a student should be approached with caution. Nonetheless, it is difficult to find a string teaching scenario wherein the teacher does not utilize pedagogical touch with permission from the student.

5. Because the primary objective of the beginning string class is proper setup and string playing is a physical activity that requires ample room to move, string teaching and playing require a space that encourages movement. Students should be able to bow freely with enough space for the teacher to be able to move among them.

So then, what does a typical beginning string classroom look like?

CLASSROOM SETUP

The teachers' ability to deliver effective instruction is determined in part by the setup of the classroom. Inadequate facilities can be detrimental to the overall morale of students and can impede instruction. An organized, spacious classroom that reflects the values of the teacher, students, and the school is desirable. A welcoming space is inclusive and representative of the students who will be taught in that space. Students respond to role models that they can relate to and who look like them. Posters and instructional materials that represent the diversity in your classroom can make students feel included or, by omission, excluded. Be conscious of the content of posters, images, and other materials that you to choose to display in your classroom as these images affect students' sense of belonging.

The location of instrument storage, music stands, visual aids, and timekeeping devices have an impact on classroom procedures and consequently, student focus. Organizing the classroom so that distractions are limited will improve classroom management and student learning. For example, arranging the room so that students who are late enter the back of the classroom, rather than crossing in front of the teacher, limits potential interruptions. Likewise, facing the students away from windows or glass doors may increase their focus during class time.

Many string pedagogues recommend setting up the beginning string orchestra classroom so that the students are seated in a box formation.[20] This seating arrangement allows the teacher to frequently change proximity to assist students individually (see Table 1.1 and Figure 1.1). Sharing stands is not recommended in a beginning strings class because the placement of the music stands interferes with the teacher's ability to move between the students who are sharing, making it difficult to assist students with their bow arm, in particular. A setup that includes ample space between students also provides an advantage for effective classroom management. As students become more advanced, they should learn how to share stands. Having a stand partner is important during orchestra rehearsals because the inside player (the person sitting away from the audience) is responsible for page turns, while the outside player (the partner sitting closer to the audience) continues playing. The following are two different seating formations for the beginning strings class.

You will notice in Table 1.1 that the violins and violas are placed to the right of the teacher rather than the left as displayed in Figure 1.1. In a traditional setup, the violins generally sit to the left of the conductor. However, if students are taught to sit correctly, the violin and viola players will orient their bodies so that the scrolls of their instruments are pointing toward the music stand (see Figure 1.2). This physical orientation provides room

Table 1.1 This Setup Places the Violins and Violas in a Location Where the Teacher Can Easily Monitor the Angle of Bow Placement and Move Throughout the Classroom.

Bass	Bass	Bass	Bass	Violin	Violin	Violin
Cello	Cello	Viola	Viola	Violin	Violin	Violin
Cello	Cello	Viola	Viola	Violin	Violin	Violin
Cello	Cello	Viola	Viola	Violin	Violin	Violin
Cello	Cello	Viola	Viola	Violin	Violin	Violin
			Teacher			

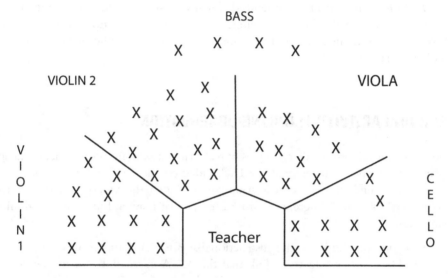

Figure 1.1 Traditional Orchestra Formation

Figure 1.2 Violin and Viola Seated Position

to bow and a direct view of the music and the teacher. By placing the violin and viola students to the right of the teacher, the angles of the students' bows are more easily viewed. If the violins and violas are seated to the left of the teacher, the teacher will need to walk to the far-left side of the classroom to assess bow angles.

Any setup is of value if the choice is deliberate and related to the instructional goals for that rehearsal or classroom period. Different arrangements are more effective for different activities. While the box formation allows the teacher to change proximity and help students individually, it does not allow students to make eye contact with one another, nor does it provide students with a clear view of the conductor. Building technique is easily accomplished within the box formation, while more collaborative activities benefit from a seating arrangement where students are able to see one another in addition to the teacher. The *ASTA String Curriculum* recommends that many musical activities occur initially without the instrument.[21] A flexible space where students are able to move one day, be seated in a box formation the next day, and have some rehearsals in a traditional orchestra set-up is most beneficial.

LEARNING ACTIVITY 1: ONLINE OBSERVATION

The following videos include examples of real string classrooms with students engaging in various types of music making. Each video contains a clear instructional goal along with a different type of classroom setup. Watch the videos and discuss the instructional goals and different classroom setups that may be found in a beginning string class:

1.1   1. What do you think are the instructional goals during this movement activity in Video 1.1? Why do you think that the ASTA curriculum recommends that beginners engage in musicianship activities away from the instrument prior to performing them with the instrument?

1.2   2. How does the activity presented in Video 1.2 relate to the previous movement activity?

1.3   3. Which recommended formation is being utilized by the teacher in Video 1.3? What do you think the teacher's primary objective is in this video excerpt? Is this formation enabling the teacher to meet her instructional goals as presented in the video?

1.4   4. Which formation is being used by the teacher in Video 1.4? What is the benefit of this arrangement in this instance?

1.5   5. What is the primary instructional goal presented in Video 1.5? What other purposes might this activity serve?

6. Traditional orchestra seating places the string players in columns rather than rows. Why is it that in a band, flutes commonly occupy the first row, clarinets the second row, and so on? Why are the first violins not all in the first row, second violins in the second row, violas in the third, and so on?

7. What other variables do you think you should consider when you set up your classroom? How much do you think the setup and classroom environment affect the students' ability to learn?

NOTES

1. National String Project Consortium. (2009). *Wanted: 3,000 string teachers!* The status of string and orchestra programs in United States Schools. American String Teachers Association, White Paper. Retrieved from www.astaweb.com/App_Themes/Public/Uploads/PDF/WhitePaper.pdf.
2. El Sistema. Retrieved from https://elsistemausa.org/.
3. Gillespie, R. A. & Hamann, D. L. (1998). The status of orchestra programs in the public schools. *Journal of Research in Music Education, 46*(1), 75–86.
4. Gillespie, R. A. (1997). String teacher training: Using history to guide the future. *American String Teacher, 47*(1), 62–66.
5. Hamann, D. L., Gillespie, R. A., & Bergonzi, L. (2002). Status of orchestra programs in the public schools. *Journal of String Research, 2*, 9–35.
6. National String Project Consortium. (2009).
7. Gay, G. (2010). *Culturally responsive teaching: Theory, research, & practice.* (2nd ed.). New York, NY: Teachers College Press.
8. Ladson-Billings, G. (1995). But that's just good teaching! The case for culturally relevant pedagogy. *Theory into Practice, 34*, 159–165.
9. Lind, R. L. & McKoy, C. L. (2016). *Culturally responsive teaching in music education: From understanding to application.* New York, NY, and London: Routledge Taylor and Francis Group.
10. Galamian, I. (1962). *Principles of violin playing & teaching.* (2nd ed.). Englewood Cliffs, NJ: Prentice-Hall, Inc.
11. Havas, K. A. (1970). *A new approach to violin playing.* (5th ed.). London: Bosworth.
12. Menuhin, Y. & Primrose, W. (1976). *Violin and viola.* New York, NY: Schirmer Books.
13. Mantel, G. (1975). *Cello technique.* (B. H. Thiem, Trans.). Don Mills, ON: Indiana University Press. (Original work published in 1972).
14. Rabbath, F. (2012). *A new technique for the doublebass.* Paris: A. Leduc.
15. Simandl, F. (1968). *New method for string bass.* S. Sankey (Ed.). New York, NY: International Music Company.
16. Rolland, P., Mutchler, M. & Hellebrandt, F. (2010). *The teaching of action in string playing.* (3rd ed.). Urbana, IL: Illinois String Research Associates.
17. Allen, M. L. (2001). A Pedagogical model for beginning string instruction: Revisited. In D. A Littrell & L. R. Racin (Eds.), *Teaching music through performance in orchestra* (3–13). Chicago: GIA Publications; Benham, S. J., Wagner, M. L., Aten, J. L., Evans, J. P., Odegaard, D. & Lieberman, J. L. (2011). *ASTA string curriculum: Standards, goals and learning sequences for essential skills and knowledge in K-12 string programs.* Fairfax, VA: American String Teachers Association; Hamann, D. L. & Gillespie, R. (2013). *Strategies for teaching strings: Building a successful string and orchestra program.* (3rd ed.). Oxford, New York: Oxford University Press.
18. Allen, M. L. (2001); Benham, S. J. et al. (2011); Green, E. A. H. (1999). *Teaching stringed instruments in classes.* Fairfax, VA: American String Teachers Association; Hamann, D. L. & Gillespie, R. (2013).
19. Behrend, L. & Keats, S. (1998). *The Suzuki approach.* Sumy-Birchard Inc.
20. Culver, B. (1989). *The master teacher profile: Elements of delivery at work in the classroom.* University of Wisconsin-Madison, Division of University Outreach, Department of Continuing Education in the Arts; Hamann, D. L. & Gillespie, R. (2013); Lamb, N. & Cook, S. L. (2002). *Guide to teaching strings.* (7th ed.). New York, NY: McGraw-Hill.
21. Benham, S. J. et al. (2011).

CHAPTER 2

Fundamentals of Teaching String Instruments

INSTRUMENT POSITION

Proper setup is one of the primary goals of a beginning string class. One may assume that proper technique and good tone are inextricably linked, and that is true for many wind instruments and supported singing. The beginning string student, however, is able to produce a quality sound and reasonable intonation for the first year of instruction utilizing a number of setups that initially feel more "comfortable" than standard pedagogical recommendations. One need only observe bluegrass, old-time, and Irish fiddlers to find individuals who possess alternate instrument positions and are highly accomplished musicians and performers. The problem with atypical setup occurs when habits form and students desire to progress across a variety of styles. Shifting, vibrato, double stops, and varied articulations required in classical, jazz, and contemporary music cannot be performed unless the student has first acquired the proper instrument position. Furthermore, injury prevention is important, and careful attention to proper setup will alleviate tension and allow for more comfortable playing.

Proper instrument position is outlined by the *American String Teachers Association National Curriculum* (2011) and is organized as follows:[1]

> **Body Format**—Students perform with a lengthened and balanced posture; support instrument without tension, demonstrate ease of motion; format is adjusted for physiological changes due to growth; control of weight distribution, unilateral movement, bilateral movement, in sitting and standing position.
> **Left Hand Skills and Knowledge**—Students perform with the correct placement and angle of the left arm-wrist-hand-fingers to the instrument; demonstrate position that is balanced and free of tension; play with independence of fingers, ease of motion and control of finger weight; produce characteristic tone with vibrato (as appropriate); show understanding and ability to apply fingerings, finger patterns, shifting, extensions.
> **Right Hand Skills and Knowledge**—Students perform with fluent bowing motion, control of variables (weight, angle, speed, and placement), in a variety of bowing techniques and articulations with characteristic tone.

Establishing the correct instrument position (including body format), left hand position, and right hand position is essential during the first year of instruction. Students are capable of producing a good sound, decent intonation, and strong rhythm skills with an array of poor technique in the initial stages of learning a string instrument because there is no causal relationship between setup and good tone. Students with excellent ears may be even more inclined to deviate from proper setup initially because they may achieve the desired musical result more easily using a different setup. In *The Master Teacher Profile*, Bob Culver (1989) explains that master teachers focus instruction primarily on proper setup during the first year of instruction.[2] That is not to say that musical skills should not be addressed! Comprehensive music instruction, such as tone, steady pulse, meter, rhythm, intonation, improvisation, composition, and music reading, should be included in the curriculum. The teacher is responsible for reinforcing the foundational skills to prevent bad habits from forming.

Why do string teachers focus extensively on proper setup?

Because proper setup sets the foundation for future instruction.

DEVELOPING MUSICIANSHIP SKILLS

Along with instrument setup, musicianship skills should be taught from the very beginning of instrumental instruction. Sound–before–sight is a foundational principle of teaching music. Prior to having students read written notation, have them experience music aurally and kinesthetically. Teach foundational musicianship skills to the students without the instruments before having them read notation with the instruments.

Pulse, Meter, and Rhythm

Maintaining a steady beat or steady pulse is an essential skill for young musicians. In fact, human beings as a general rule struggle to keep time, which is why we invest in time-keeping devices. Incorporating fun movement activities, listening activities, and games will help students develop the requisite rhythm skills. When asking students to find the pulse, consider the fact that rhythm and pulse occur in layers. Students should be encouraged to feel the macro beat (larger beat) and micro beat (smaller beat). Watch Video 2.1. You will see that the young students in this classroom are finding both the large beat (macro) and the small beats (micro or subdivisions). At no time is there a discussion of note values as that information is not yet relevant.

In addition to steady beat, differentiating between groups of twos and threes allows students to acquire the foundational skills that lead to understanding meter. Movement activities such as bouncing a ball, walking to the beat, patching your lap, conducting, or swaying are all good activities to include regularly in your lessons. Teaching students about pulse and meter conceptually will help them understand advanced time signatures later. This way the students are not misled to believe that a quarter note always gets a beat; rather, music is organized into large and small beats that are related to one another.

Beat placement is a concept that is important as students begin performing in an ensemble and following a conductor. Once students can feel a study pulse and find the downbeat, identifying specific beats will help students perform together.

Rhythm is the actual pattern that is performed while musicians maintain a steady pulse. Most methods designed to teach rhythm recommend the following sequence of instruction: (1) imitate, (2) create, (3) read, and (4) notate. This sequence encourages students to internalize rhythmic information before seeing it. Students are ready to read notation once they can keep a steady beat, repeat basic rhythm patterns, and create basic rhythm patterns. Flashcards act as effective tools when introducing music rhythm reading.

Pitch

2.4 ▶ Singing is an excellent way to develop pitch skills. Singing simple songs with lyrics and singing on a neutral syllable are good ways to work on aural skills. Movement activities that illustrate pitch contour improve students' discrimination of high and low pitches, stepwise patterns, and skips. Incorporating Kodály, Dalcroze, and Orff activities prepares students for music reading. Prior to introducing notation, students should be able to aurally identify their open strings and be able to identify that a pitch is higher or lower in comparison to another.

2.5 ▶ Pitch notation may first be introduced with iconic representations that illustrate high versus low and steps versus skips. Identifying the open strings relative to each staff will help students later connect the pitches to the instrument. Using solfège, singing note names, and singing finger numbers are all helpful activities in the beginning strings class. Flashcards are an excellent way to introduce music reading both for pitch and rhythm.

Improvising

Creating basic rhythm and melodic patterns are an excellent introduction to improvisation. Structure activities so that students have parameters within which to create. Begin with open string improvisations. Students can create their own open string motif on the first or 2.6 ▶ second day of class. "Bile Dem Cabbage" is a song that can be performed with a constant open A when in the key of D. This song provides an opportunity for students to explore rhythmic variation on a single note, then rhythmic variation within the melody.

Call-and-response activities where the teacher plays a question and the students improvise an answer can be implemented early. Simple partner activities where students engage in brief melodic conversations can lay the foundation for future melodic improvisation. Students may also be given opportunities to realize the bass lines to songs that use chord I, IV, and V by exploring which open string in the key of D major matches best with the melody.

Creating

Many pedagogues have researched creativity in young children and have found that we inadvertently and systematically teach students to be less creative. This is done through too much structure that limits imagination. Be certain to include free improvisation early 2.7 ▶ on during instruction. Students may be encouraged to explore alternate sounds on the instruments, create soundscape stories, or compose original works. Original compositions need not be notated in a traditional way. Children should be encouraged to explore all the possibilities.

There are a number of excellent resources to help teachers increase their comfort with improvisation and creativity. Empowering students as musicians includes providing opportunities to improvise, create, and compose.

PREFERRED STRING TEACHING STRATEGIES

Imitation

String teachers become experts at teaching by rote during the initial stages of instruction, modeling frequently and requesting that students imitate what they do. In fact, the most common learning theories and systems developed for music instruction share the principle that sound- before-sight is necessary for effective music instruction. Gordon,[3] Kodály,[4] Orff,[5] Dalcroze,[6] and Suzuki[7] all recommend that initial music instruction begin with listening and imitation. "Repeat after me" is frequently heard in a beginning strings class.

Some texts refer to this music teaching technique as "call-and-response," but in the truest sense, call-and-response refers to an African-American song form wherein the response is different from the call.[8] In beginning instrumental instruction, it is more accurate to describe this process as imitation because the teacher is asking the students to perform exactly what the teacher performed. In other words, the students echo what the teacher plays.

To illustrate the value of teaching and learning by rote, consider for a moment the implications of teaching a child the age of 3 how to play a string instrument. Intuition likely tells you to begin with playful rote activities and games. If we delve into why, we can turn to educational psychology for reasons to begin with rote instruction and delay music reading (or language reading for that matter). When is a child cognitively ready to begin reading or decoding? Certainly, the answer depends on the individual child, but the important point is that the ability to read develops after a child has mastered aspects of the spoken language—be it in his or her native tongue or in music. A national report of early reading literacy showed that students demonstrated stronger reading skills when they had command of the alphabet; possessed a phonological awareness of the spoken language; were able to rapidly name a sequence of letters, objects, or colors; had the ability to recall spoken information; and could complete simple writing tasks such as writing their own name.[9] The leading learning theories in music instruction recommend that children build their aural/verbal skills prior to acquiring the associated reading skills.[10] For that reason, many of the initial activities in a beginning string class are taught by rote.

Non-Verbal, Co-Verbal, and Verbal Instruction

In 1989, Bob Culver published *The Master Teacher Profile*.[11] In this book, the traits of master orchestra teachers were analyzed to provide a framework for the public school orchestra teacher. Culver illustrated how master teachers in orchestral environments utilize non-verbal and co-verbal instructions more frequently than verbal instruction and suggested that non-verbal and co-verbal modes of instruction were more effective for orchestra teaching. He defined the three modes of instruction as follows:

> *Non-verbal* strategies or "modeling the desired response using instruments, voice, gesture, a proxy model or electronic media is the most direct means of issuing information."
>
> (p. 21)

> *Co-verbal* strategies employ "modeling and other devices while offering limited verbiage to support the response."
>
> (p. 21)

2.11 ▶️   *Descriptive (verbal)* strategies "occur when the student must listen to a verbal descrip-
tion, translate that into a musical response and then produce the necessary movements to produce the sound."

(p. 21)

Using non-verbal and co-verbal instruction more frequently than verbal instruction
makes sense when one considers that approximately 93% of communication dealing with
feelings and attitudes has been attributed to non-verbal behaviors, with only 7% attributed
to the verbal content of the message.[12] Body language, eye contact, facial expressions, proximity, touch, and vocal inflection are all aspects of non-verbal communication[13] and have
been identified as important elements in effective teacher delivery.[14]

Co-verbal instruction is more prevalent in string environments than band environments,
probably because of the difference in volume produced by a beginning orchestra compared
to a beginning band. While co-verbal instruction is recommended in a string environment,
one argument against its use is the student's inability to hear what the teacher is saying.

2.12 ▶️   Co-verbal instruction is therefore best used as a prompt, or preemptive instruction that
occurs during a gap in performance, during quiet moments in performance, or during the
teacher's own modeling.[15] In addition to providing instruction while students are playing,
accomplished string players/teachers have the ability to combine verbal instruction with
modeling by describing verbally as they play. This approach can be extremely effective in
making instructions clear.

2.13 ▶️ Teacher Modeling During Student Performance

There are numerous reasons to model during student performance in a string setting:

1. Modeling a string instrument is very visual. In a professional orchestra, the string player
    is expected to know where the principal player is in the bow at all times and watches
    the principal player in addition to the conductor. Tone color, phrasing, and articulation
    can be seen to a large degree in the way that the player uses the bow. In this way, per-
    forming along with string teachers while they model is similar to watching the prin-
    cipal player, or even similar to watching a conductor, and is a skill that the beginning
    string player should acquire.
2. An advanced player (the teacher) is able to establish a strong sense of pitch and is gen-
    erally able to play much louder than an entire ensemble of beginners. This provides an
    aural target for the students.
3. Similarly, an advanced player (teacher) is able to establish a strong sense of pulse both
    aurally and visually for the students. Again, this provides a clear target that the students
    can emulate.

Modeling these aforementioned attributes is more efficient than talking about them and
thus can be more effective. There are also a number of reasons that string teachers should
not always model and play with their students:

1. While playing one's own instrument, it may be difficult to hear the students accurately.
    The performer may primarily hear oneself, thus masking the sound of the students and
    impeding the ability to assess the students' performance.
2. The students can be misled to think that they sound better than they do while the
    teacher is contributing. This is very reinforcing but does not allow the students to
    self-assess accurately.

Similar to co-verbal instruction, modeling during student performance is only effective when it is done deliberately and with the intent of meeting an instructional goal. String teachers need to discern when this is a helpful strategy and when it becomes a crutch for the students.

Modeling

Why is there a separate category for modeling? We already covered modeling! Well, yes, and no. Imitation and teaching by rote have been discussed, as well as performing with the students, but modeling can take other forms, including vocal modeling, peer modeling, piano modeling, recorded models, and so on. Asking a student to imitate a pitch pattern, rhythmic pattern, or sections of a song is somewhat different than modeling a concept, style, or phrase. Often when string teachers model a concept like tone production, they may not expect an immediate response from the students (e.g., repeat after me). Rather, they may be demonstrating so that they can ask students to attend to different elements of the music, which may include musical attributes, expression, or technique. The teacher may incorporate questions in this process or even include partner activities or discussion.

Modeling is ubiquitous in string teaching. Modeling during student performance frequently takes the place of conducting during the first year of instruction. Models other than the teacher are important, and peer modeling can be one of the most influential types of instruction. Suffice it to say that modeling is an important aspect of string teaching.

Pedagogical Touch

As was mentioned in the first chapter, manually assisting string students is a frequent instructional strategy employed by string teachers. While much of string playing is visual, there remain aspects that are more easily understood if the student can experience them kinesthetically, for example, the weight distribution and flexibility of a bow hold or the trajectory of the bow motion. As you have seen in the instructional videos online, string teachers frequently move among students adjusting their instrument setup. This frequent use of pedagogical touch relates back to the primary goal of the beginning string class—proper setup. Sometimes the proper setup required to play a string instrument is more easily taught through physical assistance. Caution must be employed when physically assisting students in the public school. Teachers should consult administration, parents, and students. Always ask students if you have their permission to help them prior to using manual assistance.

LEARNING ACTIVITY 2: METHOD BOOK REVIEW

An analysis of different method books can clarify the learning goals and sequencing of the typical string class. This activity is not intended as a method book review to assess the quality of various method books. Rather, the activity is intended as an exploration of beginning string teaching. As you analyze the books, assume that the process you are reviewing is valid and useful. The author recommends reviewing at least three different method book series. Answer the following questions and reflect on how beginning strings are similar to and different from other music classrooms with which you have had experience:

1. What information is presented in the first five pages?
2. What are the common keys and order in which the keys are presented?
3. What type of note values are introduced in the beginning? Why do you think the rhythms progress in the order presented?
4. What meters and time signatures are included? In what order?
5. How many different articulations are introduced? Which ones are introduced?
6. Are dynamics included? When are they introduced?

NOTES

1. Benham, S. J., Wagner, M. L., Aten, J. L., Evans, J. P., Odegaard, D. & Lieberman, J. L. (2011). *ASTA string curriculum: Standards, goals and learning sequences for essential skills and knowledge in K-12 string programs*. Fairfax, VA: American String Teachers Association.
2. Culver, B. (1989). *The master teacher profile: Elements of delivery at work in the classroom*. University of Wisconsin-Madison, Division of University Outreach, Department of Continuing Education in the Arts.
3. "*The Gordon Institute for Music Learning*," accessed September 14, 2017, giml.org.
4. Choksy, L. (1999). *The Kodaly method I: Comprehensive music education*. (3rd ed). Upper Saddle River, NJ: Prentice Hall.
5. Orff, C. & Keetman, G. (1950–1954, 1966). *Orff Schulwerk: Music for children*. (5 volumes). English Trans. by Margaret Murray. Mainz: Schott Music International.
6. Jaques-Dalcroze, E. (2000). *Rhythm, music, and education*. (5th ed.). Trans. by H. F. Rubenstien. London: The Dalcroze Society, Inc.
7. Behrend, L. & Keats, S. (1998). *The Suzuki approach*. Sumy-Birchard Inc.
8. Southern, E. (1997). *The music of black Americans: A history*. (3rd ed). New York, NY: Norton & Company.
9. Lonigan, C. J. & Shanahan, T. (2009). *Executive summary of the report of the national early literacy panel*. Retrieved from https://lincs.ed.gov/publications/pdf/NELPReport09.pdf.
10. Choksy, L. (1999); Gordon Institute for Music Learning (2017); Behrend, L. & Keats, S. (1998).
11. Culver, B. (1989).
12. Mehrabian, A. (1981). *Silent messages: Implicit communication of emotions and attitudes*. (2nd ed.). Belmont, CA: Wadsworth. ISBN 0-534-00910-7.
13. Knapp, M. L. & Hall, J. A. (2014). *Nonverbal communication in human interaction*. Boston, MA: Wadsworth, Cengage Learning.
14. Hamann, D. L., Baker, D. S., McAllister, P. A. & Bauer, W. I. (2000). Factors affecting university music students' perceptions of lesson quality and teaching effectiveness. *Journal of Research in Music Education, 48*, 102–113. doi:10.2307/3345569; Hamann, D. L. & Gillespie, R. A. (2013). *Strategies for teaching strings: Building a successful string and orchestra program*. (3rd ed.). New York, NY: Oxford University Press; Yarbrough, C. (1975). Effect of magnitude of conductor behavior on students in selected mixed choruses. *Journal of Research in Music Education, 23*, 134–146. doi:10.2307/3345286
15. MacLeod, R. B. (2017). The perceived effectiveness of non-verbal, co-verbal, and verbal string ensemble instruction: Student, teacher and observer views. *Journal of Music Teacher Education*, 1–15.

CHAPTER 3

Preparing Your Classroom

Young teachers and preservice teachers frequently ask, "How do you start the first day of class?" The better question may be, "What do I need to do to get ready before the first day of class?" There are many things to consider prior to beginning instruction. What ages or grades will you be teaching? How many students are enrolled in each class? Will the students provide their own instruments or will the school? How do you determine how many or what sized string instruments you will need? What instructional materials will you use? Does the school already own method books or repertoire? Do you have a budget for materials and repairs? What method book should you use, if you choose to use one? Will you be teaching the students homogeneously (with only like instruments in the class) or heterogeneously (violins, violas, cellos, and basses combined)? How many times a week will you meet with your students? How long is each instructional period?

If you are hired to fill a position that was previously occupied by another teacher, many of the preceding questions have been decided for you, and you will be expected to familiarize yourself with the structure of the program in which you will be teaching. If, however, you are starting a program from scratch, then you will need to make recommendations to your administration about budget, instruments, repairs, classroom space, starting age or grade, class sizes, instructional time, and more. There are no straightforward answers to any of these questions. String programs throughout the United States are structured in a variety of ways. The following are some basic guidelines to help you get started:

1. Budget—String programs can be expensive. If the program will provide instruments for the students, it is important to look up the cost of the instruments and include these in your budget request. Do not forget to include instruments, replacement strings, shoulder rests, rock stops, rosin, cleaning cloths, music stands, chairs, music, and a repair budget. These items are all basic necessities in a beginning strings class.
2. Instruments—String instruments come in a variety of sizes, which is explained later. Quality instruments that are the correct sizes for the students enrolled in your class are essential.
3. Repairs—Instruments may be damaged. If the program is responsible for the maintenance of the instruments, there should be an annual repair budget. Replacement strings, replacement bows (or bow rehairing), rosin, and rock stops are all necessary items.
4. Classroom space—As was mentioned in Chapter 2, there needs to be enough space that the students can move freely and the teacher is able to move among them.

Table 3.1 Recommended Class Size and Instructional Time by Age

Grade	Size Caps	Instructional Time
1st grade	6–8	2× week, 20–30 minutes
2nd grade	8–10	2× week, 20–30 minutes
3rd grade	10–12	2× week, 30–40 minutes
4th grade	12–15	3× week, 30–40 minutes
5th grade	15–30	3× week, 40–50 minutes
6th grade	20–40	5× week, 40–50 minutes

5. Instrument storage—Storing string instruments appropriately is important. Because string instruments are made of wood, humidity must be controlled. Wild fluctuations can cause seams to open or instruments to crack. Most luthiers recommend storing instruments between 60 and 80 degrees, with a controlled humidity ranging between 45% and 60%.[1]

6. Starting age—String instruction can begin as early as age 3. The younger the children, the more individualized attention they will need. The recommendations included in Table 3.1 are based on my own personal observations of effective string classrooms.

PARTS OF THE INSTRUMENTS

Familiarize yourself with the various parts of the string instruments. This information will help with instrument selection and instrument setup procedures. Referring to the parts of the instrument using the correct terminology will avoid confusion for your students. In the diagrams Figure 3.1 you can see that most of the terminology is the same across instruments. Note that the violin and viola have a chinrest, while the cello and bass do not. Likewise, the cello and bass have an endpin, while the violin and viola have an end button.

Parts of the Violin/Viola   Parts of the Cello   Parts of the Bass

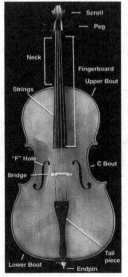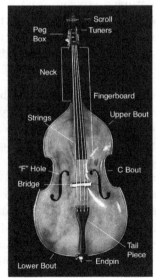

Figure 3.1 Parts of the Instruments

The Bow

The parts of the bow (Figure 3.2) are the same across the four instruments with one noted exception—the string bass may be played with either a French bow or German bow (Figure 3.3). The style of bow used to play bass is a topic of debate. Non-bassists should consult area bass players regarding the style used most prevalently in the area in which the students reside. If there are no other string players in the area to consult, teachers may choose the method that is most comfortable for them to model and for their students to play.

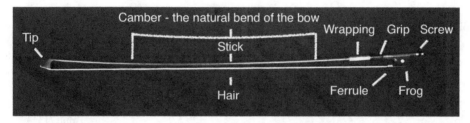

Figure 3.2 Parts of the Bow

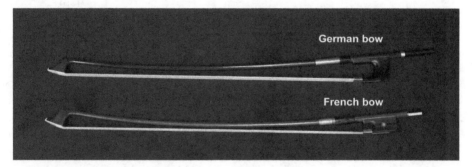

Figure 3.3 French and German Bows

INSTRUMENT SIZING

String instruments come in a variety of sizes to accommodate various body types and sizes. Learning on the correct size instrument is critical to student success. The correct instrument size may be determined using a number of approaches that take into consideration the size of the student's hand and length of the arm (violin and viola) or height, size of the hand, and length of the arm (cello and bass). When a student seems between sizes, assigning a smaller size instrument is preferred.

The following Table 3.2 outlines the typical sizes available from most instrument dealers and includes the correct body length measurement along with the approximate age of the student. In many schools, parents are invited to a recruitment session that includes sizing the students before they enroll in classes, thus ensuring that each individual student has access to the correct-sized instrument. If students cannot be sized individually prior to the acquisition of the instruments, the ages listed in the table can be used as a basic guide but are not intended to replace the individual sizing process. When purchasing a set of classroom instruments, obtain a range of sizes. Young children may experience growth spurts and can transition quickly from one size to another. For this reason, most instrument dealers will permit students to rent to own so that the money spent renting an instrument

Table 3.2 Instrument Sizes and Lengths[1]

Instruments	Size	Body Length	Approximate Age
Violins	4/4	14″	Adult (12+)
	¾	13 ¼″	10–11
	½	12 3/8″	8–10
	¼	11 ¼″	7–9
	1/8	10″	6–8
	1/10	9 ¼″	4–6
	1/16	8 ¼″	3–4
	1/32		2–4
Violas	16 ½ ⎫	16 1/2″	Adult (14+)
	16 ⎪ Full	16″	11–13
	15 ½ ⎬ Size	15 ½″	10–12
	15 ⎭ Violas	15″	
	Intermediate	14″	
	Junior	13″	
Cello	4/4	29 5/8″	Adult (13+)
	¾	27 3/8″	11–12
	½	25 ½″	10–12
	¼	21″	9–10
	1/8	17 7/8″	6–8
	1/10	16″	5–7
Double Basses	4/4	45 ½″	Generally not used
	¾ (considered full	42 ½″	Adult (14+)
	size)	40″	12+ (including small
	½	37 6/16″	adults)
	¼		9–12

[1] *The Complete String Guide: Standards, Programs, Purchase, and Maintenance.* (1988); Music Educators National Conference.

accrues toward the purchase of a full–size instrument. Many dealers will place a limit on the amount of money that may be accrued toward this purchase.

Teaching Advice: Work with your area music dealer to make sure that they are providing the sizes that you want for your classroom. Be aware that the body length measure does not include the neck and scroll. A full-size violin should measure 14″.

Teaching Advice: Frequently, students will arrive to your class with an instrument belonging to a relative. This instrument may be too large for the student. Educating the parents about safety and the potential for injury when playing an instrument that is too large is critical to the student's success. Common performance injuries include carpal tunnel, ganglion cysts, tendonitis, and strained muscles.[2] Encourage parents to rent a smaller size instrument until the student can safely play the full-size instrument.

Sizing the Violin and Viola

The most common method used to determine which size violin or viola a child should play is to place the instrument into the approximate playing position and have students extend their arm the length of the instrument and attempt to wrap their fingers around the scroll and into the peg box.

Three common criteria for correct sizing include the following:

1. The length of the arm—Students should be able to extend their arm and reach around the scroll into the peg box
2. A 90-degree angle forms in the left arm when the left hand is placed in playing position in the first position (violin only).
3. The size of the left hand should allow students to comfortable place each of their fingers onto the finger tapes in first position.

Sizing the Cello

There are two common methods for sizing the cello. The first is based on the size of the student's left hand. In playing position, the student should be able to reach comfortably from first to fourth finger in first position (see Chapter 5). The second method considers the size of the student's body in relation to the cello. The student also needs the correct size chair so that the top of the thigh makes a 90-degree angle with the lower leg. The endpin should be extended such that the lower bouts of the cello are in line with the knee, the heel of the neck lies approximately over the heart, and the C-peg falls behind the left ear.

Ideally, both methods are used to determine the proper size cello. The body and hand should be comfortable so that students can move freely as they learn to play. When in doubt, the smaller size is the better choice.

Sizing the Bass

The standard size double bass for an adult is a ¾ size. Rarely is a true full-size bass played. To determine the correct size string bass, one must take into account the student's height, arm length, and hand size. Bass pedagogy is the most diverse of the string instruments and includes more than one philosophy and perspective. There are many suggestions for how to set up the beginning bassist, and the author has chosen to present the most thorough approach that takes into account the various perspectives:

1. Determine the appropriate bass height for the student. Raise the endpin so that the student's second knuckle from the fingertip of the right hand is in line with the bridge of the bass.
2. Have the student place his or her left hand into first position. The first finger should be approximately at eye level. If the first finger is above eye level, try a smaller size bass. If the first finger is below eye level, select the next size higher.
3. With the student's left hand in first position, make sure that the hand can easily span a whole step (fingers 1, 2, 4) without straining. The hand size may require a smaller bass.

PREPARING THE INSTRUMENTS

String instruments should be assessed and prepared prior to beginning instruction. Cultivating a strong relationship with area music dealers can alleviate many maintenance and preparation issues that otherwise may fall to the teacher. Whether it is the responsibility of the string teacher or the music dealer, the instruments and bows need to be in good working condition.

Tuning

Tuning is one aspect of string instruction that can occupy a substantial amount of instructional time if the teacher is not efficient. Tuning may need to be done more than once prior to the first day of instruction so that the instruments will hold their pitch during the first week of classes. Experienced string teachers spend approximately 6 minutes tuning their beginning string class each instructional period.[3] Time must be devoted to tuning so that students obtain discerning pitch skills, but time spent tuning is also instructional time that may be lost. Efficiency is extremely important when motivating and retaining students, as well as maintaining a focused and engaged environment. Tuning the instruments prior to the start of classes will help set the tone for the rest of the year. Quality instruments will help the teacher avoid many issues throughout the year.

> **Teaching Advice:** To expedite time spent tuning, many teachers will only tune the strings that will be used in class that day. Sometimes it is more important to begin instruction than it is to get everyone's instrument perfectly in tune. Prepare warm-up activities that promote student leadership so that the teacher may float and tune while students lead a warm-up. Improvisation exercises on open strings can be used as a learning task for students while the teacher moves throughout the classroom tuning.

Finger Placement Markers

Most experienced string teachers who teach in group settings recommend the use of finger tapes or dots to help establish correct left-hand position. There are a number of ways to apply finger placement markers (see Chapter 5). Some manufacturers even supply finger tape markings preset in the approximate distance needed for the fractional size instruments. Other pedagogues choose to use a color-coded system where the various colors corresponded to specific notes and are consistent across the instruments.

LEARNING ACTIVITY 3: BUDGET PROPOSAL

1. What are some things that you need to consider prior to the first day of classes at a new job?
2. How will you prepare the instruments?

3.   How will you know what size instruments you may need?
4.   What other issues do you think you will need to consider prior to the first day of class?
5.   You have been hired to teach orchestra and the administration of your new school has asked you to submit a budget. Create a proposal to include instruments, music, and music stands for 50 new orchestra students.

NOTES

1.   Sweetman, N., Glanville, D. & Gilles, N. (2016). Ask the experts. *The Strad*, February, 66-67. Retrieved from www.thestrad.com/ask-the-experts-how-effective-are-instrument-case-humidity-gauges/510.article.
2.   Wilke, C., Priebus, J. C., Biallas, B. & Frobose, I. (2011). Motor activity as a way of preventing musculoskeletal problems in string musicians. *Medical Problems of Performing Artists*, *26*(1), 24–29.
3.   MacLeod, R. B. (2010). A comparison of instructional strategies used by experienced band and orchestra teachers when teaching a first year class a new line of music. *Bulletin of the Council for Research in Music Education*, *185*, 49–62.

CHAPTER 4

Instrument Position

Proper instrument position is essential to student success on a string instrument. As was explained in Chapter 2, a decent tone and respectable intonation can be achieved during the beginning stages of instruction without proper setup. Intermediate and advanced skills, such as double stops, shifting, and vibrato, however, cannot be executed without proper instrument and left-hand position. Students will be unable to produce a variety of articulations without a balanced and flexible bow hold. For these reasons, string teachers should carefully teach and reinforce good technique from the first lesson. Beginning string method books generally introduce the correct instrument position first (which includes body format as addressed in the ASTA Curriculum);[1] then introduce either left-hand activities (pizzicato) or right-hand activities (bowing open strings). Choosing to introduce the left hand prior to the right hand or the right hand prior to the left hand is simply a matter of preference, and either sequence can be effective. Regardless of whether the teacher begins with right-hand or left-hand activities, separating skills during beginning instruction is recommended.[2]

REMOVING THE INSTRUMENTS FROM CASES

Rest low string instruments on their sides to protect the sound post[3] that is inside the body of the instrument (see Figure 4.1).[4] Placing the low string instruments on their sides reduces the potential for the sound post to become loose and fall out. Before removing the cello and bass instruments from the cases, take the bow out of the front pocket of the case so that it is not damaged during the unpacking process. Once the bow is in a safe place, the students may unpack the cellos and basses being mindful of the bridge. Instrument cases should be placed under student chairs or to the side of the room so as not to block the teacher's ability to move about the classroom.

Violin and viola players should get on the floor with their instrument before opening their instrument cases. Opening the cases while seated or kneeling on the floor reduces the possibility that the instrument may fall during the unpacking process. Ensure that the instrument cases have the correct size facing up before allowing the students to open them. Generally, the

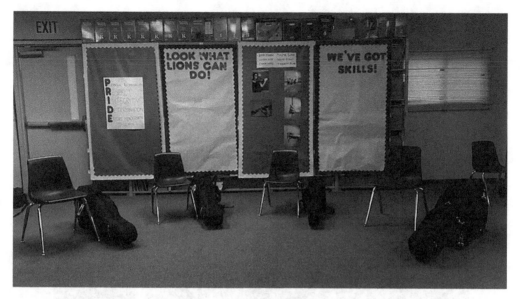

Figure. 4.1 Properly Placing the Cellos on Their Side Within the Soft Case

thinner part of the case is the top. Once all instrument cases are flat and the correct side is up, students may open the cases, remove the violin or viola, and return to their seat.

Teacher Advice: Instruments can be damaged on the first day if precautionary steps are not taken. What may seem like common sense to an experienced player is unknown to the beginning student. If the students open the cases upside down in their lap during the unpacking process, it is likely that at least one student will drop the instrument. Removing bows from the cello and bass cases prior to unpacking the instrument will protect the bow from being damaged as students set their cases aside.

VIOLIN/VIOLA INSTRUMENT POSITION

Guitar Position

Once the instruments are safely out of the cases, have the students sit on the edge of their chair with their feet flat on the floor. Initially, it may be more efficient to have the violin and viola players hold their instruments in "guitar position." In guitar position, the instrument is visually positioned like a seat belt. There are two important checkpoints for guitar position (see Figure 4.2):

Guitar Position Assessments:

1. The scroll of the instrument should be in line with the left shoulder.
2. The back of the instrument should be flat against the student's upper body.

Figure 4.2 Guitar Position

Shoulder Position

Some teachers prefer to teach violin and viola in shoulder position from the beginning. The size of the group or the age of the students can influence this choice. For example, in large heterogeneous groups with slightly older students, guitar position can be extremely effective because this position is easily attained and more time can be focused on the cello and bass instrument positions. With very young students, however, the left-hand skills learned in guitar position may not automatically transfer to shoulder position, and young students may become confused. If the teacher chooses to begin in guitar position, students should move to shoulder position as soon as it is convenient.

Shoulder rests are commonly used to help support the violin or viola on the shoulder. The use of shoulder rests is sometimes controversial. Some teachers believe that the instruments should be supported without the use of these devices. Others believe strongly in using raised chinrests, sponges, or other implements. The purpose of a shoulder rest, sponge, or raised chinrest is to reduce the distance between the chin and the chinrest so that the player's head is in the most natural position possible. Finding the correct setup for each individual student is very important to avoid injury, reduce tension, and ensure their success on the instrument.

Many shoulder rests allow the height to be adjusted. To determine the correct height of the sponge, shoulder rest or chinrest, have the student place the violin or viola on their shoulder and measure the distance between the top of the chinrest and jaw. The goal is to decrease this distance so that the jaw may be placed comfortably on the chinrest. Chinrests typically contain nickel, and some students may be allergic. To prevent allergic reactions from these students, the teacher can cover the chinrest with a cloth, moleskin (which can be purchased at a convenience store), or some type of gel or soft padding. There are many devices to consider when placing violin and viola students in shoulder position. The most important thing is that they are comfortable and can support the weight of the instrument for limited amounts of time without the use of their hands. Finding a comfortable setup may take time, so encourage patience.

Sequencing Instruction for Shoulder Position

1. Establish the correct feet position: hip width apart with the left foot ever so slightly in front of the right foot (Figure 4.3). Movement helps establish the correct body format, including a lengthened spine, balanced posture, and unlocked knees. Have students frequently sway back and forth transferring their body weight from the left to right foot or bend their knees and "bounce." A relaxed position is more easily attained through movement.

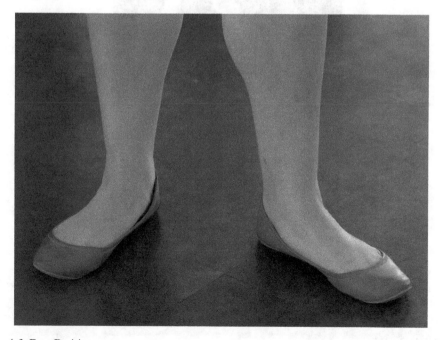

Figure 4.3 Feet Position

2. Have the students hold the violin firmly with two hands. One hand should be placed on the heel of the neck, and the other touching the end button (Figure 4.4).

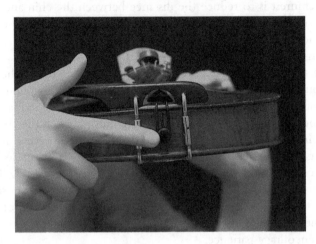

Figure 4.4 End Button

3. Raise the violin above the head and sway back and forth (Figure 4.5). This swaying motion loosens the muscles and squares the shoulders to prepare for the violin or viola.

Figure 4.5 Raised Violin

4. Lower the violin or viola at an angle with the scroll slightly higher than the chinrest. Make sure that the violin is placed onto the student's collarbone with the end button placed to the center or left of the hollow in the student's throat before the student places their jaw onto the chinrest (Figure 4.6).

Figure 4.6 Placement of the End Button

5. Double-check that students are not raising their left shoulders to support the instrument. Shoulders should remain relaxed (Figure 4.7).

Figure 4.7 Relaxed Shoulders

6. Practice holding the violin without the support of the left hand for brief periods of time. Swing the arms to encourage a relaxed motion (Figure 4.8).

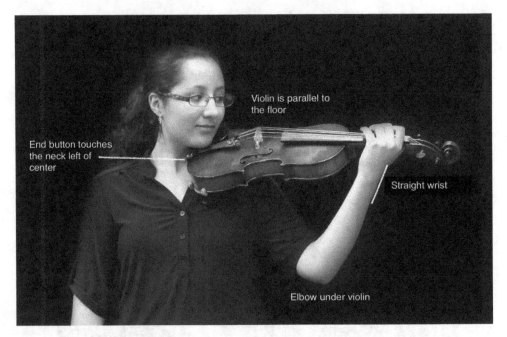

Figure 4.8 Violin and Viola Position

Violin and Viola Position Assessments

1. Feet are hip width apart, weight is evenly distributed, and knees are soft and relaxed.
2. The violin/viola can be held without hands, free of tension for a brief time.
3. The violin/viola is parallel to the floor with a slight slope (E string lower than G string or A string lower than C string).
4. The end button is to the left of the hollow in the student's throat.
5. The jaw is placed comfortably on the chinrest.

CELLO INSTRUMENT POSITION

When in a seated position, the student's upper legs should be parallel to the floor and feet should be just beyond shoulder width apart (see Figure 4.9). Some students' feet will need to extend farther forward or backward to achieve the desired position. The height of the chair may even need to be adjusted, which is why many professional cellists can be seen using a piano stool to perform as soloists. Piano stools are generally adjustable. Most music classrooms will have standard sized chairs. In elementary classrooms it is important to have a variety of chair sizes to accommodate different sized students.

Sequencing Instruction for Cello Instrument Position

1. Have students extend the cello endpin so that the cello is approximately at eye level when the student is standing. This endpin length is only an approximation and will likely need to be adjusted once the student is seated.

Figure 4.9 90 Degree Angle in the Legs and Approximate Endpin Height at Eye Level.

2.   The students should stand with feet slightly wider than shoulder width apart and ex-
     tend the cello one arm's length away from themselves.
3.   Place the endpin such that it creates an equilateral triangle with the student's feet.
4.   Have the student sit toward the front of the chair; then bring the cello back to the left
     side of the body.

Cello Position Assessments

1.   The endpin should make an equilateral triangle with the student's feet.
2.   The heel of the cello neck should fall over the student's heart, or just to the left of the
     student's heart. Some teachers align the heel of the neck with the student's sternum.
3.   The C-peg should be behind the student's left ear with a fist-sized space between the
     neck of the cello and the student's shoulder.
4.   The lower bouts of the cello should be around knee level.

Figure 4.10 Cello Position with Checkpoints

Teaching Advice: At this juncture, experienced cellists generally desire to provide more information about proper setup. While that information is important, it is inadvisable to give the students any more to think about at this time; otherwise, they may become overwhelmed. Also, remember that in a heterogeneous classroom, the students assigned to other instruments have been sitting patiently waiting.

BASS INSTRUMENT POSITION

There are two schools of thought regarding bass setup: sitting or standing. One method utilizes a stool; the other has the player stand while holding the bass. In both methods, the proper bass height must be determined.

Standing Position

Many bassists prefer to stand because they find the position more comfortable or feel that they can get a more powerful sound in this position. Public school teachers should understand how to correctly teach standing position because many districts may not provide stools.

Sequencing Instruction for Standing Position

1.   Have students position the bass upright with the bridge directly in front of the student, as if the bass and the player were dance partners (see Figure 4.11).
2.   Have students relax their right arm and measure the distance from the second knuckle of the right hand to the bridge. The endpin should then be extended that distance.

Figure 4.11 Determining Bass Height

3. The bassists' feet should be shoulder width apart with the left toe pointing to the left.
4. With the endpin extended, position the bass so that the endpin is slightly to the left of students' left foot an arm's length away from the students' body.
5. Rotate the bass slightly so that the back of the upper bout will rest along the left pant inseam. Students can now lean the bass toward themselves.
6. Double-check that the players' first finger is approximately eye level (see Figure 4.11).

Bass Assessments for Standing Position

1. The student's bow arm should be able to reach to the bridge.
2. The first finger of the left hand should be approximately eye level in first position.[5]
3. Feet should be shoulder-width apart, flat on the floor, and relaxed with the left foot just slightly forward and turned out.
4. The bass should rest in the student's left pant inseam.
5. The right-lower bout comes in slight contact with the inside of the left knee.
6. The student should be able to balance the bass with no hands or allow the instrument fall slightly forward (see Figure 4.12).

Seated Position

Some bassists prefer using a stool to play because they find it more comfortable and feel that they have more facility in this position. When students attend honors festivals and are required

First finger
eye level

Student is able
to balance the
bass without the
use of the hands.

Bass rests
in the inseam
of the left
pant leg

Feet shoulder
width apart

Endpin
location

Figure 4.12 Bass Standing Position

to play for many hours in succession, stools can be very important. Any standard bar stool will work for seated position. For students who are playing on ¾ size instruments, which is typically considered the adult–sized, the standard stool height is 29″ or 30″. For smaller students, it is advisable to cut the legs of the stool to a more appropriate length to allow for correct posture. Bass stools should be the height that allows the player to rest on the stool rather than sit on it.

Sequencing Instruction for Seated Position

1.   With both feet flat on the floor, have the student sit on the front half of the stool. The left leg will then be placed on the rung of the stool which is most comfortable for the student (see Figure 4.13).

Figure 4.13 Bass Body Format in Seated Position

2. To determine the correct instrument height, measure the distance from the second knuckle of the right hand to the bridge while the student is seated. The bridge of the bass should be facing the student.
3. With the endpin extended, place the bass an arm's length away with the endpin to the left of the player's stool.
4. Rotate the bass so that the back of the upper bout will rest along the left pant inseam. The student can now lean the bass toward themself (see Figure 4.14).
5. Some players prefer the bass to rest in the right pant inseam. This depends on the individual player and their bass.

Figure 4.14 Supporting the Bass

Bass Assessments for Seated Position

1. The student's bow arm should be able to reach the bridge.
2. The nut of the bass should be around the height of the student's forehead.[6]
3. The back-left side of the upper bout should contact the student's left or right pant inseam.
4. The student should be able to balance the bass in playing position without the aid of the left hand (see Figure 4.14).

First finger eye level

Back
lower bout
rests
in left
pant inseam

Right
hand
reaches
bowing
lane

End pin
location

Figure 4.15 Bass Seated Position

INTRODUCING THE OPEN STRINGS

Tuning

Tuning a large class of beginning string players is challenging for any music teacher. Famil-iarize yourself with the open strings of each instrument (see Figure 4.16). String instru-ments need to be checked for tuning prior to each lesson and every practice session because the pitch can vary widely. Beginning students are not yet prepared to tune during the first

Figure 4.16 Notation for the Open Strings

several weeks of instruction, sometimes during the entire first year, because, in addition to learning how to match pitch, students must also learn how to physically move the tuning pegs. The string teacher is responsible for quickly and efficiently tuning the class at the start of each lesson. Installing fine tuners on beginner instruments is strongly recommended. Both student and teacher will benefit from having fine tuners because they allow small changes in the pitch of the strings and are much easier to physically manipulate compared to the pegs. If you as the teacher are just learning to tune, do not be afraid to double-check yourself with an electronic tuner. Ultimately, string teachers and players need to develop acute pitch discrimination skills, but in a large classroom, efficiency is important, so technological tools are encouraged.

Teaching the Open Strings

The first open string activities are taught by rote: modeled by the teacher and repeated by the students. Violin, viola, cello, and bass share three stings in common: A, D, and G (see Figure 4.16). Focusing on these three strings initially will keep everyone engaged. Also, in the key of D major, these open strings provide the roots to the tonic, dominant, and subdominant chords, allowing students to harmonize from the first lesson. Students should not look at the notated exercises until after the open strings have been learned. Emphasizing aural skills from the beginning will engage the students' ears and allow them to focus their attention on proper setup and pizzicato technique.

4.1 ▶ **Open String Activity 1: Introduce the Open Strings Pizzicato—**

An efficient method to introduce the open strings is to have students echo the teacher performing each string. Figure 4.17 is a notated exercise that teachers may use to introduce the students to open strings by rote. Video 4.1 includes an example of students learning the open strings using this method.

After the students can successfully imitate rhythm patterns performed by the teacher on the open strings, have the students recall the location of the strings to reinforce the open string names. For example, the teacher may sing, "One, two, pluck the A." The students respond by plucking the name of the string called with a predetermined rhythm. This activity frees the teacher to walk around the room and assist students with proper instrument position and pizzicato tone (see Figure 4.18).

4.2 ▶ **Open String Activity 2: Recalling the Open String Names and Sounds**

Ear training is important to develop from the very beginning. Have students aurally find their open strings. In this exercise, the teacher performs open strings without naming them

Figure 4.17 Introducing the Open Strings

Figure 4.18 Recalling the Open Strings by Name

and has the students identify the string aurally to repeat the pattern they hear. The notated activity shown in Figure 4.18 is only an example to illustrate the process. The sequence of open strings should be varied so that students are using their ears to match what they hear (see Figure 4.19).

Figure 4.19 Recalling the Open Strings by Ear

4.3 ▶ Open String Activity 3

4.4 ▶ Once students have memorized the open strings, have them create their own open string motif. Ask students to play a melody using only the open strings (see Video 4.4). Additionally, there are a number of fun open-string songs for younger aged children. Some teachers will have the students perform "Open String Concertos" with improvised piano accompaniment by the teacher. The open strings can be easily accompanied by adding a I–V–I chord pattern using the open string as the fifth scale degree. Included here are two open-string songs that are exciting and fun for young students to play (see Figures 4.20 and 4.21).

OPEN-STRING SONGS

Teaching Advice: Figure 4.20 shows is an original tune designed to teach open strings, rhythmic improvisation, and introduce students to the concept of swing and the blues. The eighth notes should be swung. Remember that students should not yet look at notation. Have students improvise a variety of rhythms on the open strings.

> **Teaching Advice:** Introducing diverse music to your students from the very beginning is important. This open-string song is a West African song, "Nampaya Omame" (see Figure 4.21). Parts 2 and 3 are introduced in the next chapter. This open-string song should also be taught by rote. Although the rhythm looks challenging to read, students can successfully perform this rhythm rather quickly when taught by rote. The percussion parts can be played on shekere and djembe instruments or by tapping on the bodies of the string instruments.

Open String Blues   arr. Blanton

Figure 4.20 Open String Blues Arranged by Blanton

Nampaya Omame

Figure 4.21 Nampaya Omame Open String Part

LEARNING ACTIVITY 4: WRITE A LESSON PLAN

As a teacher, memorizing the open strings is essential. Review open-string activities 1, 2, and 3; then answer the following questions:

1.   What are the open strings of the violin from low to high?
2.   What are the open strings of the viola from low to high?
3.   What are the open strings of the cello from low to high?
4.   What are the open strings of the bass from low to high?
5.   Which strings do all three instruments have in common?
6.   What do the violin and bass have in common? What is different about the tuning of the string bass compared to the other three instruments?
7.   How do you think the similarities and differences between the open strings of the four instruments impact sequencing and instruction?

8. If the majority of beginning strings method books start students in the key of D, what types of foundational music activities can the students perform using only the open strings?

Write a brief lesson plan

1. Review the content knowledge you have acquired about proper instrument position. Write a brief 10-step procedure to assist a student in getting the instrument safely out of the case and into playing position.
2. Explore some beginning string method books or go online to find fun songs or games to teach the open strings. Write a brief lesson plan to teach your open-string song to the class or to a friend.
3. Teach a friend how to hold the string instrument that you are currently learning. Write a brief lesson plan that includes the objective (proper instrument setup), procedure (minimum of 10 steps), and assessment (specific checkpoints that you can visually assess that are aspects of proper instrument setup).

NOTES

1. Benham, S. J., Wagner, M. L., Aten, J. L., Evans, J. P., Odegaard, D. & Lieberman, J. L. (2011). *ASTA string curriculum: Standards, goals and learning sequences for essential skills and knowledge in K-12 string programs*. Fairfax, VA: American String Teachers Association.
2. Allen, M. L. (2001). A pedagogical model for beginning string class instruction: Revisited. In D. Littrell & L. R. Racin (Eds.), *Teaching music through performance in orchestra*, Vol. 1. (3–13). Chicago: GIA Publications.
3. The sound post is a dowel rod that is located inside of string instruments. The sound post serves the dual role of transmitting vibrations between the top plate and bottom plate of the instrument as well as supporting the top of the instrument.
4. McKean, J. (2016). The role (and romance) of the bass bar. *Strings*. Retrieved from http://string smagazine.com/the-role-and-romance-of-the-bass-bar/.
5. If you find it difficult for students to meet both checkpoint 1 and 2, refer to Chapter 3. The instrument may be too large for the student, and selecting a ½-size or ¼-size bass may help.
6. If you find it difficult for students to meet both checkpoint 1 and 2, refer to Chapter 3. The instrument may be too large for the student and selecting a ½-size or ¼-size bass may help.

CHAPTER 5

Developing the Left Hand

String players associate a number with each of the left-hand fingers. The index finger is 1, the middle finger 2, the ring finger 3, and the pinky 4 (see Figure 5.1). The thumb is referred to as "thumb." Students should memorize the number associated with each finger. Body mapping different parts of the left hand will help students understand teacher instructions and will increase awareness of how to shape the different parts of their hand as it relates to the instrument. Become familiar with each knuckle joint (fingertip, first knuckle, second knuckle, and base knuckle joint).

Although the violin and viola have some differences that impact how one plays the instrument, there are enough similarities that these two instruments are addressed together in this chapter. Addressing the violin and viola simultaneously as frequently as possible increases pacing and benefits the entire class.

FINGER PLACEMENT MARKERS

Most experienced string teachers who teach students in groups recommend the use of finger tapes or dots to help establish correct left-hand position. Finger placement markers are controversial because some teachers and performers fear that students will use their eyes rather than their ears to locate the correct pitch, thus impeding their ability to develop good intonation and aural skills. Good intonation on a string instrument is not concrete—meaning that the pitches are only in-tune in relation to the surrounding context. For example, leading tones are played slightly higher on a string instrument, which means that an F# in G major will be performed higher than an F# in D major. This level of sophistication is important for more advanced players. Training students to discriminate good intonation is one of the most important skills they will develop as string players. However, the margin of error that can occur with 20 or more individuals is much greater than what may occur in a one-on-one setting and far exceeds the difference between F# in D major and F# in G major. For that reason, many teachers use finger tapes as an aid for developing both the left-hand frame and a solid foundation for pitch.

Finger placements markers may be placed in a variety of different ways. Paul Rolland recommended placing one finger marker to indicate the octave note and a dot to indicate the halfway harmonic[1] (see Figure 5.2). Dr. Suzuki recommended finger placement markers

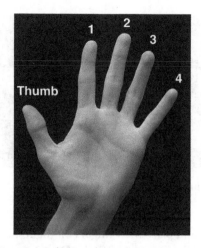
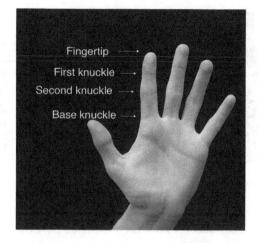

Figure 5.1 Labeling the Left–Hand Fingers

Figure 5.2 From Left to Right, Suzuki Finger Tapes and Rolland Markers

to assist the mother when practicing with her child and generally includes a marker for fingers 1, 2, 3, and 4.[2] Some manufacturers even supply finger tape markings preset in the approximate distance needed for the fractional size instruments. Other pedagogues choose to use a color–coded system where the various colors corresponded to specific notes and are consistent across the instruments.

SHAPING THE LEFT HAND

Violin/Viola

The following sequence may be used to shape the left hand in either guitar or shoulder position. There are advantages to both approaches (see Chapter 4, "Instrument Setup").

1. Have the students begin in guitar or shoulder position.
2. The students should identify the "crease" of their left hand, which is located near the base knuckle joint of the index finger (see Figure 5.1).
3. Have students slide their hand up and down the neck of the instrument while maintaining contact with the base knuckle joint of their index finger. As the hand slides, the wrist should remain straight (Figure 5.3).

Figure 5.3 Hand Slides Up and Down the Fingerboard While Touching the Crease of the Base Knuckle Joint

4. Ask students to rest their left hand near the scroll and place their fingers on the respective tapes. Beginning tapes are generally set in the finger pattern for the D major scale. Place fingers 1, 2, and 3 on the tapes so that the highest note sounds D on the A string.
5. Rest the thumb across from, or slightly behind, the first finger.
6. The left-hand fingers should be placed on the violin string so that the inside corners hold down the string and the fingernails face toward the low string side of the bridge (see Figure 5.4).

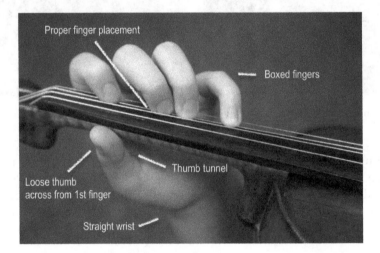

Figure 5.4 Finger Placement on the String

7. The left-hand fingers should make a box shape. Some students may need to adjust where the index finger contacts the side of the neck. The base knuckle joint may be too high or too low depending on the size of the student's hand (see Figure 5.5). Double-check that students' fingers are boxed.

Violin/Viola Left-Hand Assessments

1. The index finger should contact the neck of the violin or viola such that the student's left-hand fingers are boxed.
2. The fingers are placed on the string so that the "inside corners" hold down the string.

DEVELOPING THE LEFT HAND

3. The left–hand wrist is straight.
4. The thumb is loose and placed across from the first finger.
5. A space exists between the neck of the violin and the thumb joint of the hand (thumb tunnel).

Figure 5.5 Boxed Fingers

Cello/Bass

The cello and bass have some similarities. The following sequence is intended to create the most efficient pacing possible in a heterogeneous classroom. Address the cellists and bassists together when teaching elements that are common between the two instruments.

1. The left hand of the cello and bass resembles the shape of an imperfect *C* (see Figure 5.6). Have students create a *C* with their left hand as shown in the photo below while maintaining a straight wrist.

Figure 5.6 Left Hand in *C* Shape

2. Imagine holding a grapefruit, a water balloon, or a can of soda. These are good examples of the proper shape of the left hand. As you imagine holding the can of soda, notice that the thumb naturally rests behind the second finger.
3. The wrist should remain straight while students practice making the correct hand shape.

Cello

1. Transfer the *C* hand shape to the A string of the cello, aligning the left-hand fingers with the finger placement markers. Place fingers 4, 3, 2, and 1 down on the corresponding finger markers.
2. Tap the thumb behind the second finger slightly to the left side of the neck to prevent squeezing.
3. The wrist should be straight and the elbow at a comfortable height that enables students to slide their left hand up the string towards the bridge without touching the body of the instrument (see Figure 5.7).

Figure 5.7 Left Hand Shape on the A String

Bass

1. Make a circle with the thumb and second finger while maintaining a straight wrist.
2. Open the circle into the C-shape and place the second finger of the left hand on the G string over the C# finger marker. Rest the thumb gently on the neck of the bass behind the second finger.
3. Place fingers 3 and 4 down together so that the fourth finger is on the top finger marker. The index finger should extend back one-half step and rest on the bass. This left-hand position is called the K-position (see Figure 5.8).
4. During beginning instruction, bassists do not use their third finger in isolation; rather, they use fingers 3 and 4 together to increase strength.[3]
5. The wrist should be straight and the elbow at a comfortable angle that will allow students to slide their left hand up the string towards the bridge.
6. Unlike the other string instruments, in order to play the D major scale, bass players must shift from third to first position. Maintain contact between the second finger and the G string to slide the hand back to first position (see Figure 5.9).

Figure 5.8 Bass Left Hand K-position

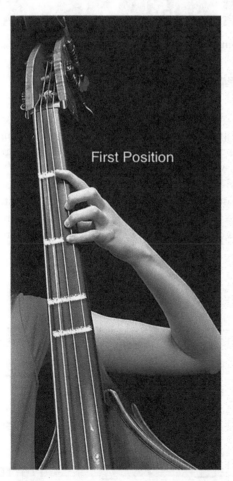

First Position

Third Position

Figure 5.9 First and Third Position on the Bass

Cello/Bass Left-Hand Assessments

1. The left-hand fingers are boxed.
2. The wrist is straight or gently bent.
3. The fingernails are facing the adjacent string.
4. The thumb loose and behind the second finger.
5. Cello: The fingers are equidistant apart.
6. Bass: the hand is shaped in K-position (see Figure 5.10).

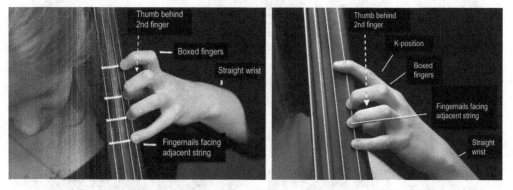

Figure 5.10 Cello and Bass Left Hand Position from Left to Right

ESTABLISHING THE LEFT HAND FRAME

The left hand should be balanced and free of tension. Beginners will benefit from placing all fingers down on the string in a block hand position rather than placing only one finger down at a time. Building the hand frame with all the fingers down serves two pedagogical purposes: (1) It promotes good hand position with fingers that hover close to the fingerboard when not in use to prevent "fly away fingers." (2) It creates a kinesthetic reference for the space between the intervals on the instrument, thus establishing more consistent intonation from the beginning. Many method books will introduce the left hand using a descending scale. The activity shown in Figures 5.11 through *5.14* should be taught by rote.

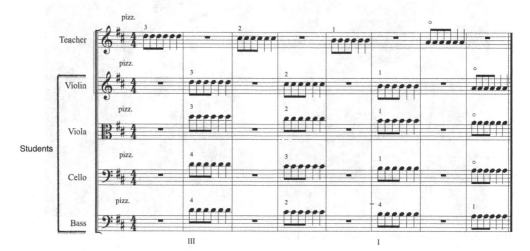

Figure 5.11 Descending D Major Tetrachord (upper)

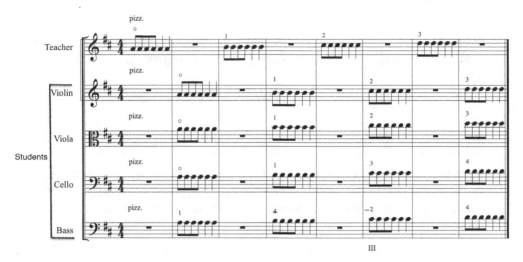

Figure 5.12 Ascending D Major Tetrachord (upper)

Figure 5.13 Descending D Major Tetrachord (lower)

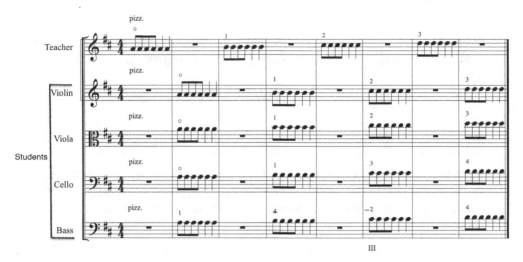

Figure 5.14 Ascending D Major Tetrachord (lower)

Note: From the very early stages of instruction in a heterogeneous group, the basses will need to shift. For a detailed explanation of fingerings, refer to the bass chapter.

Teaching Advice: Once the left hand has been set up on the A string for violin, viola, and cello, it is a simple transfer task to repeat the same process on the D string. The bass utilizes a slightly different pattern, but the first-position hand frame and pattern are consistent.

5.1

5.2

Teaching Advice: If the students began with the violin and viola players in guitar position, they should now be transitioned to shoulder position and the preceding activities repeated. Shoulder rests, raised chinrests, or sponges are all devices designed to make shoulder position more comfortable. The teacher should explore the option that is best for each student. Acquiring the correct shoulder position that is comfortable for each student is essential for all future success on the instrument. The importance of establishing the proper shoulder position from the beginning cannot be overstated.

Freedom of Motion

In 1974, Paul Rolland developed *The Teaching of Action in String Playing*.[4] This project incorporated movement activities from the beginning of instruction that increased string players flexibility and freedom of motion. One of the fundamental principles of proper setup on a string instrument is the ability for students to support the instruments without the assistance of the left hand. Having the left hand free allows players to shift, vibrate, and move their fingers with increased dexterity.

5.3

Teaching Advice: Pinky strums free the left hand and shoulder joint, strengthens the pinky, and teaches correct elbow height for the different strings. Have students strum from the lowest to highest string (see Figure 5.15 *and Video 5.3*). The elbow should swing right to left while the left hand maintains the proper shape.

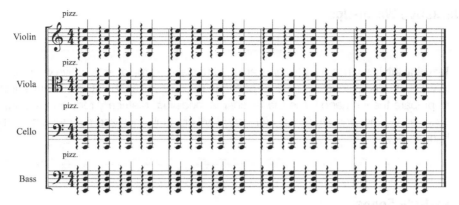

Figure 5.15 Pinky Strums (Rolland, 2010)

Teaching Advice: Another exercise that frees the left hand is D Scale in Canon (see Figure 5.16). After performing the pizzicato measures, the students should tap the rhythm on their right shoulder with their *left* hand. This activity requires students to release their left hand and support the instrument with their head. On cello and bass, crossing the left hand over the neck of the instrument to touch the right shoulder encourages the proper instrument position, with the neck of the instrument close to the student's head and body.

Figure 5.16 D Scale in Canon

Interactive Warm-Ups

Teaching Advice: Once the students are able to play in D major, interactive warm-ups in which students echo the teacher continue to be useful as the students have time to prepare the left hand while the teacher is modeling. Metrically reducing the time between teacher and student performance will gradually increase the students' left-hand facility.

Three-Note Songs

Teaching Advice: It is not necessary to learn the entire D major scale prior to introducing three-note songs. In fact, the earlier students can perform songs, the more motivating practice may be. Using the first three scale degrees in D major allows basses to play three-note songs without shifting (see Figure 5.17).

Figure 5.17 Hot Cross Buns

Teaching Advice: Once students have learned the harmony to "Hot Cross Buns," have them pizzicato the bass line with their *left*-hand pinky (see Figure 5.18). Plucking with the left-hand pinky will help correctly shape the left hand position for violin and viola, as well as strengthen the pinky for all four instruments.

Figure 5.18 Hot Cross Buns Bass Line

Teaching Advice: Students may now work in groups to create their own arrangements of Hot Cross Buns utilizing these three parts while simultaneously working on left hand shape, intonation, and pizzicato tone.

You can teach open-string bass lines for any beginning three-note song.[56] Bass lines that use only the roots of the chords (open strings) are a wonderful way to begin teaching students how to audiate harmony. Using solfège or scale degrees, teaching students that *do* and *mi* are accompanied by a I chord and *re* by a V chord is an excellent introduction to harmonic understanding. Find and learn at least five three-note songs on your own and realize the harmony. All music teachers should increase their knowledge of simple three-note songs.

Teaching Advice: *Bring Me Little Water Silvie* is an African-American work song of which the origin is unknown, but the song is frequently attributed to Lead Belly, African-American folk singer and blues musician. *Silvie* is strophic in form, meaning the melody repeats with different lyrics on each refrain. The song is notated in Figure 5.19 so that violin and viola have the melody and the cello and bass perform the bass line. All instruments should be given the opportunity to perform both parts. Additionally, basic improvisation and arranging can be introduced with this song, including introductions, lead-ins, echoes, and harmonization. An example of students performing their own arrangements of this song can be viewed in Video 5.4.

5.4

Figure 5.19 Bring Me Little Water Silvie

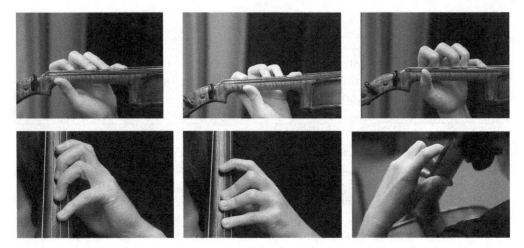

Figure 5.20 Common Issues Found in Left-Hand Setup

LEARNING ACTIVITY 5: CHOOSE ONE OR MORE OF THE FOLLOWING TEACHING ACTIVITIES

1. Teach the left-hand warm-up routine presented in this chapter. Be able to model for the class proper instrument setup and good pizzicato tone.
2. Teach a friend proper left-hand setup. Design a brief lesson plan with objectives, procedures, and assessments. Then teach someone to play the descending D or G tetrachord and a simple song. Take a photo or video of the finished product to show your teacher and assess your student's performance.
3. Design your own interactive warm-up to develop left-hand skills in the key of D major (pizzicato only).
4. Teach a simple three- or five-note melody by rote.

Explain the left-hand setup issues in the photos in Figure 5.20 and provide suggestions as to how these issues may be solved.

NOTES

1.   Rolland, P., Mutchler, M. & Hellebrandt, F. (2010). *The teaching of action in string playing.* (3rd ed.). Urbana, IL: Illinois String Research Associates.
2.   Behrend, L. & Keats, S. (1998). *The Suzuki approach.* Sumy-Birchard Inc.
3.   Simandl, F. (1968). *New method for string bass.* S. Sankey (Ed.). New York, NY: International Music Company.
4.   Rolland, P. et al. (2010).
5.   Learning Together by Winifred Crock, William Dick, and Laurie Scott has many simple unison melodies with open string bass lines.
6.   Crock, W., Dick, B. & Scott, L. (2010). *Learning together: Sequential repertoire for solo strings or string ensemble.* Sumy-Birch Inc.

CHAPTER 6

Developing the Right Hand

The most important element of a good bow hold is flexibility. A flexible bow hold allows players to produce a variety of articulations and avoid performance-related injuries. Whether the teacher focuses primarily on left-hand activities or right-hand activities during initial instruction is a matter of preference. Regardless of the presentation order in any method book, the author believes that the bow hold should be taught as early as possible, preferably on the first day of instruction.

> **Teaching Advice:** Initially the bow hold should be developed on a cylindrical object such as a pencil, straw, or spaghetti noodle. Using a straw provides kinesthetic feedback to students if they squeeze. The following activities should be done first without the bow and then repeated with the bow.

FORMING THE BOW HOLD

Violin/Viola Bow Hold

1. Begin by relaxing the right hand. Allow the hand to hang naturally. The thumb should be behind the second finger or between the first and second finger.
2. Draw an imaginary line (if permissible, use chalk or washable marker) through the student's right hand 1.5 knuckles deep and at a slight diagonal to indicate where the stick of the bow (or straw) will contact the right hand (see Figure 6.1).
3. Have the students hold an imaginary jar of salt and rotate their right hand so that the imaginary salt will fall into their lap. This motion will naturally pronate the hand and raise the elbow into the correct position (see Figure 6.2).
4. Roll the right hand onto the bow beginning with the index finger contacting the straw along the diagonal line.
5. Perch the pinky on top of the straw in a curved position.
6. Bend the thumb and contact the straw with the inside corner of the thumb (see Figure 6.3).

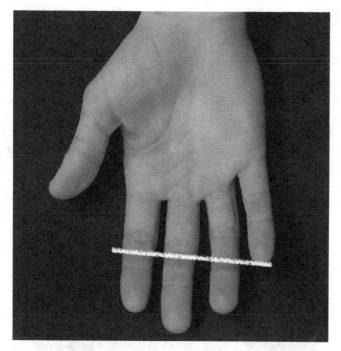

Figure 6.1 The Angle at Which the Stick of the Bow Contacts the Right Hand

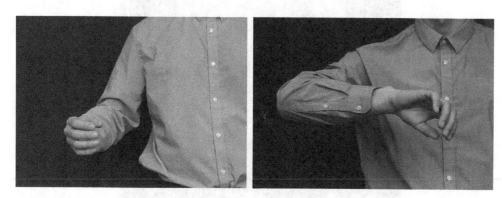

Figure 6.2 Pronation of the Right Hand

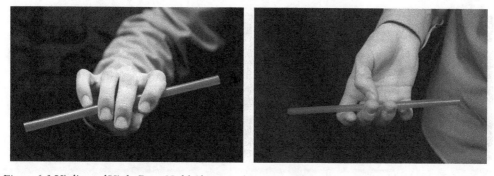

Figure 6.3 Violin and Viola Bow Hold Shape and Position of the Thumb

Cello/Bass—French Bow Hold

1. Begin by relaxing the right hand. Allow the hand to hang naturally. The thumb should be behind the second finger or between the first and second finger.
2. Draw an imaginary line (if permissible use chalk or washable marker) through the right hand 1.5 knuckles deep, one pad deep on the pinky. Note that the angle of the line is different for the cello and bass compared to the violin and viola (see Figure 6.4).
3. Place the index finger, middle finger, and ring finger approximately 1.5 knuckles deep on the straw. The pinky gently curves and hangs over the straw one pad deep.
4. Bend the thumb and contact the bow with the inside corner of the thumb. The thumb of the cello and bass is slightly less bent than the violin and viola players' thumbs (see Figure 6.5).

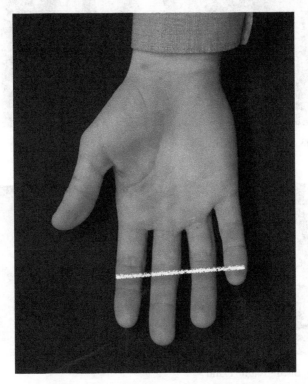

Figure 6.4 Point Where the Stick of the Bow Contacts the Right Hand for Cello and Bass

Figure 6.5 Bow Hold Shape on a Straw

Bass—German Bow Hold

1. Have the students place the heel of the bow in their right hand.
2. Place the thumb on the top of the bow.
3. With the thumb on top of the stick, make a circle with the index finger.
4. Allow the middle finger to rest at the top of the frog just under the stick.
5. The ring finger stays relaxed and the pinky curves gently under the ferrule (see Figure 6.6).

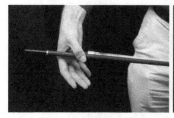  

Figure 6.6 German Bow Hold

Teacher Advice: Flexibility exercises are extremely important and should be incorporated from the beginning. While the bow hold is taught in a specific shape, in reality the bow hold is in constant motion. The shape of the bow hold changes as the hand and fingers guide the bow. Using the bow hold on a straw, increase flexibility by completing the flexibility exercises on page **XX**. Many of these exercises should be completed on a straw before holding the bow so that students receive kinesthetic feedback while performing the exercises (see thumb crunches, pinky taps, finger pull-ups, windshield wipers, and simulated bow motion).

TRANSFERRING THE BOW HOLD TO THE BOW

Teaching Advice: There are two main schools of thought on beginning bow holds. The Suzuki method has the beginning student hold the bow at the frog but positions the thumb underneath of the frog.[1] Placing the thumb under the frog provides a very young student with more control (see Figure 6.7).

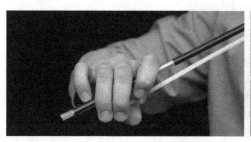 

Figure 6.7 Suzuki Beginning Bow Hold

The Rolland method begins by having young students hold the bow at the balance point rather than the frog (see Figure 6.8).[2] This method redistributes the weight of the frog to reduce tension and increase flexibility.

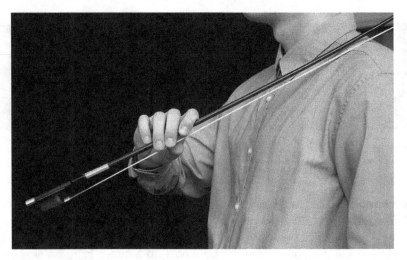

Figure 6.8 Rolland Beginning Bow Hold

Ultimately, the student will use a traditional bow hold at the frog, with the thumb contacting the stick of the bow just outside the frog's mouth. These two beginning bow holds are intermediary steps, much like training wheels on a bicycle.

COMMON ELEMENTS AND CHECKPOINTS

Repeat the preceding procedures and activities with the bow hold at the frog. Students' hands are different sizes, so instructions that are overly specific regarding where to place each finger on the bow can be counterproductive and cause tension. The most important thing is for the hand to be relaxed, balanced, and flexible.

Violin/Viola Bow Hold Assessments

1. The bow hold is approximately 1.5 knuckles deep for the index and middle fingers.
2. The thumb is flexible and in a bent position just outside the frog's mouth.
3. The middle finger hovers near the ferrule.
4. The hand is pronated, leaning slightly toward index finger.

5. The base knuckles are flat.
6. The pinky is curved on top of the bow (see Figure 6.9).

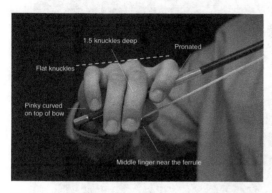 

Figure 6.9 Violin and Viola Bow Hold Checkpoints

Cello/Bass (French) Bow Hold Assessments

1. The bow hold is approximately 1.5 knuckles deep for the index and middle fingers.
2. The thumb is flexible and in a bent position.
3. The middle finger hovers near the ferrule.
4. The hand is square with the pinky approximately one pad deep (see Figure 6.10).

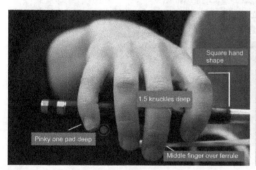 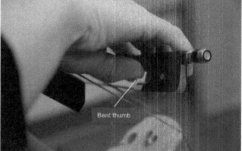

Figure 6.10 Cello and Bass Bow Hold Checkpoints

Bass (German) Bow Hold Assessments

1. The index finger and thumb complete a circle and connect on the top of the bow.
2. The heel of the bow is near the palm of the hand.
3. The middle finger to rest at the top of the frog just under the stick.
4. The ring finger stays relaxed and the pinky curves gently under the ferrule (see Figure 6.11).

One common misconception relates to the thumb and its location on the bow stick. In general, the thumb should be placed outside of the frog's mouth (see Figure 6.12). The thumb counterbalances the weight of the bow and must remain flexible.

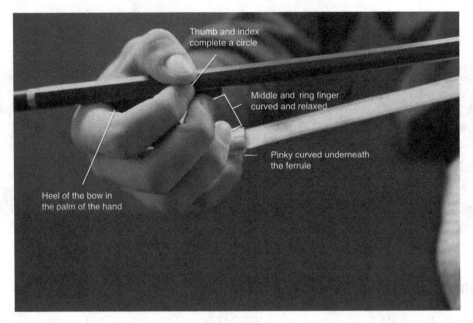

Figure 6.11 German Bow Hold Checkpoints

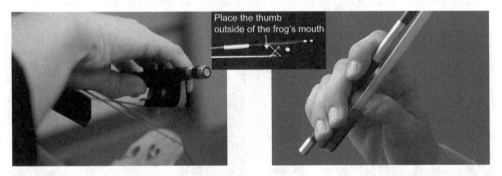

Figure 6.12 Placement of Thumb on the Bow Stick

FLEXIBILITY EXERCISES (INFLUENCED BY ROLLAND, MUTCHLER, & HELLEBRANDT, 2010)

Daily practice to increase flexibility can dramatically improve students' bow holds and tone. Many of the following exercises can be performed with the bow or another cylindrical object, such as a straw or dowel rod.

1. Thumb crunches: Repeatedly bend and straighten the first knuckle of the thumb.
2. Pinky taps: Simply tap the pinky on the bow to promote relaxation throughout the hand.
3. Windshield wipers: Begin with the bow horizontal to the floor. Using only the wrist, rotate the bow 180 degrees while maintaining a round pinky and a bent thumb. Repeat this exercise 10 times.

4. Life Saver game: Place a Life Saver on the tip of the student's bow. With the bow perpendicular to the floor, raise and lower the bow. Bend the wrist so that the bow remains perfectly straight throughout the entire motion, and the Life Saver remains on the tip of the bow.

5. Finger pull-ups: Extend and recover the fingers by pulling the bow back into the hand.

6. Spider walk: Crawl the fingers up and down the full length of the bow stick. The bow should remain perpendicular to the floor.

7. Silent rainbows: Place the bow onto the strings and silently roll from the low strings to the high strings and back.

8. Place and lift: Practice placing the bow onto the string with a round bow hold in various places in the bow (frog, middle, and tip).

9. Water pump: While holding the tip of the bow with the left hand, use the right hand to pump the bow in an up-and-down motion.

10. Rocket launch: Begin with the bow in a position perpendicular to the floor. Using only the fingers, lift the bow.

11. Rock and roll: Place the bow on top of the bridge at the frog on the low string side of the bridge; then rotate the bow so that it rolls to the high string side of the bridge. Return to the original position. Notice how the hand shape changes as you do this activity.

12. Simulate bowing: Loop the left-hand fingers around the stick of the bow and move the bow with the right hand. Concentrate on having the right-hand fingers be flexible.

Additional Recommended Activities

1. Demonstrate the bow hold on students' extended finger so that the students can feel the correct weight and lack of tension required in a good bow hold.

2. Have the students form their bow hold on the teacher's finger so that the teacher can feel the shape, weight, and lack of tension in the students' hands.

3. Have the students' right hands ride the bow to encourage flexibility.

4. Partner activities that allow students to help one another assess their bow holds.

Teaching Advice: Disguised repetition is essential when building foundational skills. Use fun activities and games to motivate students to repeatedly form their bow hold. If students cannot hold the straw using the correct bow hold, it is unlikely that they will be successfully holding the bow correctly. Imaginative teachers will find many ways to motivate their students to succeed. Watch the Video 6.13 to see students working on their bow hold.

LEARNING ACTIVITY 6: BOW HOLD ASSESSMENT

Complete one or more of the following teaching activities:

1. Teach a friend the bow hold: Design a brief lesson plan with objectives, procedures, and assessments. Then teach someone to hold the bow correctly. Take a photo of the finished product to show to your teacher and assess.

6.4
6.5
6.6
6.7
6.8
6.9
5.10
5.11
5.12
5.13

2. Lead flexibility exercises: Design a brief warm-up to include some of the flexibility exercises in this chapter. Be sure to tell the students the purpose of each activity as they are doing the activity.
3. Practice assessing and providing feedback about student bow holds online at www.routledge.com/9780815368670.

NOTES

1.   Suzuki, S. (2018). *Suzuki violin school*. Volume 1 (Rev. ed.). Van Nuys, CA: Alfred Music.
2.   Rolland, P., Mutchler, M. & Hellebrandt, F. (2010). *The teaching of action in string playing*. (3rd ed.). Urbana, IL: Illinois String Research Associates.

CHAPTER 7

Tone Production

A beautiful tone is at the center of good instrumental music instruction. Along with proper set-up, good tone should be one of the main objectives in a beginning strings class. Achieving a beautiful tone on a string instrument requires (a) a flexible and balanced bow hold, (b) the proper arm motion to produce a bow stroke that moves parallel to the bridge, and (c) an understanding of the three variables that impact tone production: bow speed, bow weight, and contact point.

THE BASICS

Once students have acquired a flexible and balanced bow hold (see Chapter 6), rhythm patterns may be performed on open strings. Before students place the bow on the string, teachers should briefly review the parts of the bow and teach students how to tighten and loosen the bow hair, as well as how to apply rosin. Violin and viola players must be able to support the instrument in shoulder position before the students are able to perform the open strings with the bow. The position of the instrument will affect students' ability to bow with proper motion. Review instrument positions before bowing open strings (see Chapter 4).

Rosin

Originally resin from pine or maple trees, rosin is a sticky substance that is applied to the bow hair so that the hair may grip the string.[1] Violin, viola, and cello rosin are solids and become powder when applied to the bow. Bass rosin, however, is stickier and "melts" onto the bow. To apply rosin to the violin, viola, and cello bow, simply tighten the bow hair and pull the bow in long, even motions up and down the cake of rosin five to six times. Apply bass rosin by moving the bow quickly in only one direction. The speed creates friction that melts the rosin onto the bow. Moving the bow in only one direction prevents the bow hairs from being pulled out by the stickiness of the rosin. Rosin should be applied regularly. Eventually, students will be able to feel when the bow does not have enough rosin.

> **Teaching Advice:** Initially, students may need a way to visually check that they have enough rosin. One approach is to draw the bow hair quickly across the thumbnail. A thin white line will appear if there is enough rosin. Too little rosin and no line will appear; too much rosin will result in a thick line. The bass bow cannot be assessed in this manner and can only be tested on the string. The bass bow should easily grab and release the string.

BOW MOTION

A proper bow motion has a balanced, flexible bow hold; moves parallel to the bridge; and remains halfway between the fingerboard and the bridge. The first bow motion should be taught unmeasured (without pulse) so that students can focus on the correct bow arm movements without additional parameters.[2] Imposing pulse and timing may result in undue tension in the bow arm. Allow students time to bow freely using the middle portion of their bow while the teacher floats to assist individuals. Isolating the middle portion of the bow increases students' success in achieving a bow motion that is parallel to the bridge.[3] Students can perform a drone while the teacher or more advanced student performs a melody.

Bowing tubes are an excellent way for students to simulate the proper bowing motion prior to placing the bow on the string. Bowings tubes can be made out of any cylindrical object through which the bow may safely move. Many teachers use decorated paper towel rolls or PVC pipe. Dowel rods are also a useful tool and can be used in place of the bow to simulate the bow motion.

7.1 ▶
7.2 ▶
7.3 ▶

> **Teaching Advice:** Many method books include an exercise called "Rosin Rap." Exercises such as these instruct the students to perform various rhythms on their cake of rosin. Be careful not to over rosin the bow! Switching from the rosin to a bowing tube is important so that students do not apply too much rosin. Bass players should use the bowing tube rather than rosin, as bass rosin is too sticky and will pull out the bow hair. View Videos 7.1-7.3 for a demonstration of the proper bowing motion for each of the instruments.

One additional parameter is whether the bow hair should be flat or tilted. Some pedagogues advocate that the bow hair remains flat with the stick of the bow directly above the bow hair; others prefer to teach the bow with the hair slightly rotated so that the stick of the bow angles towards the scroll[4] (Figure 7.1), while still others teach that the player must be able to do both.[5] All these are valid approaches. Deference to the experienced teachers in the area is one way to choose. Make sure to ask those who teach in the community which approach they prefer so that instructions for the students are more consistent.

Figure 7.1 Flat or Rotated Bow Hair

BOW PLACEMENT

Bow placement describes the placement of the bow on the string in relation to the frog or tip. There are five general areas along the bow that guide bow placement: the frog, the balance point, the middle, the upper half, and the tip (see Figure 7.2).

Have students begin playing in the middle of the bow, the area that extends from the balance point to the upper half; then gradually expand to the outer areas of the bow. The middle area of the bow is easier for a novice to control. In general, cello and bass players initiate bow strokes closer to the frog because their strings are thicker and require more weight. Because the frog is the heaviest part of the bow, initiating the bow stroke closer to the frog helps low string players create enough resistance to produce a good tone. Bassists and cellists also use a slightly slower bow speed (or less bow) with the bow placement closer to the frog than do violin and viola players. If you compare the length of violin, viola, cello, and bass bows, you will find that the low strings have a bow that is shorter and heavier than the upper string players. This is because low string instruments require more weight and slower bow speed to produce a good tone compared to their upper string colleagues.

Producing a long tone on a string instrument requires a good deal of bow control. Before students attempt to play a sustained note from frog to tip, they should explore the lower and upper half of the bow using small bow strokes. Placement exercises that have the students pick up the bow and place at the frog, balance point, middle, upper half, and tip while demonstrating a bow that is parallel to the bridge can help students feel how the arm changes position throughout the bow stroke (see Figure 7.3).

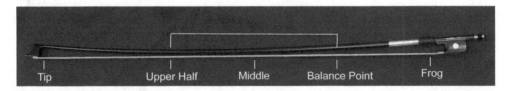

Tip   Upper Half   Middle   Balance Point   Frog

Figure 7.2 Five General Areas Along the Bow

BOW DISTRIBUTION

Bow distribution is a fundamental concept in tone production that helps students understand how to manage bow speed,[6] and works in tandem with bow placement. Bow distribution is often expressed as "spending," using more bow, or "saving," using

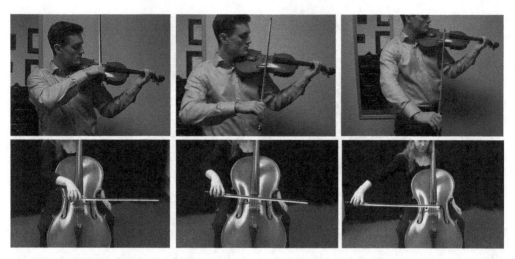

Figure 7.3 Bow Placement at the Frog, Middle, and Tip

less bow. String players need to plan ahead in order to distribute their bow logically. First and foremost, good bow distribution requires the ability to execute a consistent bow speed.

Consistent bow speed is fundamental in achieving quality tone during the beginning stages of instruction.[7] The initial rhythms patterns introduced to a beginner should include quarter notes and eighth notes in even groupings (see Figure 7.4) or sixteenth and eighth notes in even groupings depending on the tempo. Even groupings allow students to use consistent bow speed. Some teachers prefer to begin with sixteenth and eighth notes because it minimizes the amount of bow needed while also encouraging a slightly faster bow speed.

Figure 7.4 Examples of Even Rhythm Patterns

Uneven patterns are more difficult for a beginning string student because these rhythms require an uneven bow speed or cause the student to begin every other measure up-bow. These rhythmic figures should only be introduced after the students can successfully perform even rhythm patterns. Uneven patterns include dotted-half notes and dotted-quarter notes (see Figure 7.5).

Beginners should perform the following rhythms on open strings and focus on (1) using a flexible bow hold, (2) using consistent bow speed, (3) bowing parallel to the bridge, and

Figure 7.5 Examples of uneven rhythm patterns

(4) maintaining the bow halfway between the bridge and the fingerboard. The following is a typical rhythm sequence that promotes good bow technique:

1. **Rhythm Pattern 1.** Even groups of eighth notes minimize the amount of bow needed and allow students to be more successful in achieving a "straight bow stroke" or bow stroke that remains parallel to the bridge (see Figure 7.6). Violins and violas should perform this rhythm in the middle of the bow focusing on opening and close the elbow joint in the right arm. Cellos and basses should perform the eighth notes as the balance point focuses on opening and closing the shoulder joint in the right arm.

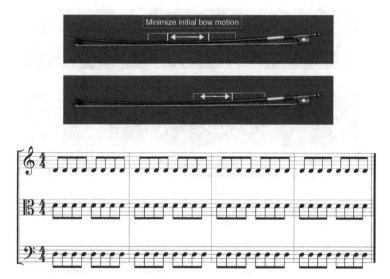

Figure 7.6 Bow Placement for Rhythm Pattern 1

2. **Rhythm Pattern 2.** Even quarter notes require the same bow arm motion as eighth notes but use twice the amount of bow (see Figure 7.7). Again, attempt to maintain a good bow hold, consistent bow speed, straight bow, and stay halfway between the bridge and the fingerboard.

3. **Rhythm Pattern 3.** Now students may begin combining the smaller bow stroke with the longer bow stroke. To play this with a beautiful sustained sound, the player needs to use a consistent bow speed. The quarter notes require twice the amount of bow as the eighth notes if the bow speed is consistent (see Figure 7.8).

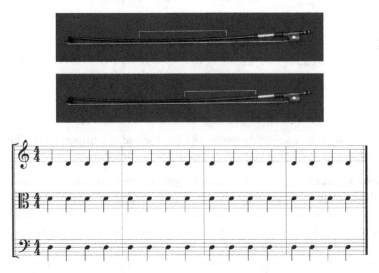

Figure 7.7 Bow Placement for Rhythm Pattern 2

Figure 7.8 Bow Placement for Rhythm Pattern 3

4. **Rhythm Pattern 4.** The bow should travel so that the first two eighth notes are played in the upper half of the bow; then the next two eighth notes are performed in the lower half of the bow (see Figure 7.9). Remember to play the rhythm with a sustained tone. Different articulations require different types of speed.

Figure 7.9 Bow Placement for Rhythm Pattern 4

Once the concept of bow distribution using consistent speed has been established, this concept can be applied to all even combinations of quarter and eighth notes on both the A and D strings. At this point, we may begin performing in the outer ranges of the bow, including the frog and the tip.

LEARNING ACTIVITY 7A: TONE EXERCISE

Bow parallel to the bridge. Practice bowing quarter notes on open strings with a partner to explore activities and strategies that will help you attain a bow motion that remains parallel to the bridge. Make a list of common issues that you think may occur with your students. Then make a list of learning tasks that help you or your partner produce a bow motion that is parallel to the bridge. Discuss what you found in class.

Practice proper bow distribution. Perform the four basic rhythm patterns outlined previously and determine how much bow to use for each note value.

THREE VARIABLES OF TONE PRODUCTION

From a physics perspective, tone production on a string instrument is produced by a combination of static friction and dynamic friction. The bow hair sticks to the string pulling the string in the same direction as the bow (static friction); then the string is released and moves the opposite direction from the bow, returning to its resting position (dynamic friction).This action occurs repeatedly, creating a continuous sound.[8] String players manipulate three variables to produce a good tone: bow speed, bow weight, and contact point.[9]

1. *Bow speed* refers to how fast or slow the bow is moving. Sometimes bow speed is also described in terms of the amount of bow being used. For example, an instruction such as "Play these quarter notes with more bow" will generally encourage the player to use a faster bow stroke. Given the same tempo and instructed to "play these quarter notes with less bow" encourages players to use a slower bow. Manipulating bow speed is often referred to as "bow distribution" and is essential to good tone production. Beginners are encouraged to use a consistent bow speed, but as players advance, different articulations, dynamics, and expression will require string players to vary the bow speed to produce the desired effect.

2. *Bow weight* is the amount of force[10] that the player applies to the bow. From a scientific perspective, force is what applies pressure or weight to the string. As a general rule, string players avoid the word *pressure* or *force*, as these terms tend to promote tension. Rather, string teachers and players prefer the word *weight* or *arm weight*. In order to achieve a constant tone, the player needs to increase weight as the bow approaches the tip and decrease weight when approaching the frog. This change in weight is necessary to offset the naturally heavier weight of the frog and lighter weight of the tip.

3. *Contact point*, sometimes called sounding point, is the placement of the bow in relation to the bridge. Initially, the contact point is eliminated as a variable in most teaching methods by asking beginning students to maintain their contact point halfway between the bridge and the fingerboard. As players advance, again, it becomes necessary to explore a wider range of contact points to increase expressive options. In order to play with dynamics, string players must be able to adjust their contact point. The contact point is also largely responsible for producing different tone colors.

These three variables (speed, weight, and contact point) work together to produce a quality tone on string instruments. In order to understand how these three variables impact tone, consider tone quality on the following continuum.

| Airy Tone | Good Tone | Choked Tone |

Musical context frequently determines the contact point as well as how much speed and weight are necessary to produce a good sound. The three variables are linked such that changing one variable requires a simultaneous change in *at least one* other variable.[11] For example, a passage may require more bow speed to produce a fuller open sound. Assuming that the player already has a good tone, the increased bow speed requires the player to either use more weight or move the bow away from the bridge. Using the continuum of airy tone, good tone, and choked tone, examine how each of the variables impact tone quality (see Table 7.1).

The reason that the good category seems ambiguous is because there is no "correct" answer. Given the context, the player may need to use more or less bow, more or less weight, or place the contact point close to or farther from the bridge. We examine each variable next.

Bow Speed

"The first principle of tone production is for it to be based on [the] speed of the bow, not pressure" (Fisher, 2012 p. vi). Consistent bow speed should be established from the

Table 7.1 Tone Quality Continuum as Impacted by Speed, Weight, and Contact Point

Variable	Airy	Good	Choked
Speed	An airy sound may be caused by too much bow speed.	Correct amount of bow speed	A choked sound may be caused by too little bow speed.
Weight	An airy sound may be the result of not enough arm weight.	Correct amount of weight	A choked sound may result from too much weight.
Contact Point	Playing too close to the bridge can cause the upper harmonics to speak, resulting in "squeaking sounds."	Correct contact point	A choked sound occurs when the player is using too much weight too far from the bridge. The player may unintentionally hit more than one string at a time.

very beginning.[12] Advanced players vary the speed for expressive purposes, but initially beginners need to learn to control the bow by producing a consistent speed. This is why many teachers provide tapes on the bow to encourage students to use more bow on quarter note values and less bow on eighth- and sixteenth-note values. The purpose of using visual markers on the stick of the bow is to provide clear goals for even bow distribution. Teachers often introduce a martelé bow stroke after students are able to demonstrate consistent bow speed. Martelé is a faster bow stroke that grabs the string at the initial attack. Suzuki teachers frequently have students say, "Mississippi, Stop, Stop," in time to indicate that the bow stops to allow a resonant ring between the quarter notes (see Figure 7.10). (See Video 7.4.)

Longer note values are introduced after students can demonstrate a controlled sound with consistent bow speed and basic martelé stroke. Long, slow bows are difficult for beginners to execute because these notes require slow, controlled bow speed and require that the player has the ability to adjust the contact point of the bow closer to the bridge. Avoid introducing long tones before students are able to produce a good and even tone on quarter and eighth notes. Long tones, however, are an excellent way to explain how bow speed varies because half notes and whole notes require the bow to slow down, which cannot be done without changing the other two variables. If students are able to produce the four even rhythm patterns using consistent speed and then a martelé bow stroke, generally they will be able to more complex rhythms and articulations.

Figure 7.10 Initial Martelé Bow Stroke on Mississippi, Stop, Stop

Bow Weight

Strictly speaking, weight is the amount of force that the player applies to the bow in order to excite the string. As was previously mentioned, string teachers use the word *weight* to reduce the potential for tension in the student's bow arm. The amount of weight needed is dependent on speed and contact point, as well as on the intended sound. Less weight will generally produce an airy sound. As arm weight increases, the sound becomes more focused. Too much weight produces a choked or crunchy sound.

The player must learn how to adjust the weight from frog to tip to create an even sound. The frog of the bow is naturally heavier than the tip, so the player must increase the amount of force as the bow approaches the tip in order to compensate for the natural weight of the bow. Rolland (2010) recommends exercises to explore producing the same tone quality in various parts of the bow (frog, middle, and tip). Try playing the example in Figure 7.11 at a constant dynamic, with the same articulation, and same tone quality in different parts of the bow.

When one considers arm weight, it is equally important for students to be able to produce a consistent sound when beginning on either an up-bow or a down-bow. In order for these two strokes to sound the same, the player must use more weight starting up-bow and less weight when starting down-bow. Perform the exercise shown in Figure 7.12 beginning each measure down-bow. Then repeat the exercise beginning each measure up-bow.

Figure 7.11 Short Bow Strokes Performed in Various Parts of the Bow

Figure 7.12 Perform this Exercise with All Down Bows. Repeat Performing Up Bow

Contact Point

The contact point, or sounding point, is the most difficult for the player to control and is usually only manipulated by more experienced players. Many pedagogues divide the area between the bridge and fingerboard into five areas, or contact points (Flesch,[13] Fischer).[14] Changing the contact point is essential to performing with different dynamics, in different registers, and with different colors. Here are some general principles about where to place the contact point:

1. *Principle 1:* Move the bow closer to the bridge when performing *forte* passages and away from the bridge to perform *piano* passages.
2. *Principle 2:* Move the bow closer to the bridge when playing very long tones (in other words, using a slow bow) and farther from the bridge to play with a faster bow.
3. *Principle 3:* Move the bow closer to the bridge when playing on higher strings and away from the bridge when playing on lower strings.
4. *Principle 4:* Move the bow closer to the bridge when playing in higher positions and on higher strings and away from the bridge when playing in lower positions and on lower strings.

The following activities will allow you and your students to experience these tone production principles firsthand. Before dividing the area between the bridge and fingerboard into five lanes, imagine that there are only three bowing lanes (see Figure 7.13). It will be easier for beginning and intermediate players to practice using three lanes before trying to incorporate five lanes. Bowing lane 1 is closest to the bridge, bowing lane 2 is halfway between the bridge and fingerboard, and bowing lane 3 is just over the fingerboard.

Figure 7.13 Three Basic Bowing Lanes

Figure 7.14 Practice Playing Quarter Notes in Each Bowing Lange to Change Dynamic Level

Now apply *Principle 1*: Play *forte* passages closer to the bridge and *piano* passages away from the bridge. Perform the quarter notes *forte* by moving the bow into lane 1. Then play the quarter notes *piano* by moving into lane 3. Use the same amount of bow for both the *forte* and *piano* passage to eliminate speed as a variable (see Figure 7.14).

Did you notice that you changed the weight when you attempted to play *forte* and *piano*? In all likelihood, you added weight to perform *forte* and used less weight to play *piano*. This activity helps the player understand that weight and contact point are linked. When players use more weight, typically, they need to move the bow closer to the bridge to support the increased weight. Try using more weight but play over the fingerboard in lane 3. What happened when you tried to use more weight over the fingerboard? You probably produced a choked sound and hit multiple strings. In general, *forte* passages are performed closer to the bridge.

Try another activity to help you understand *Principle 2:* Slower bows are performed closer to the bridge and faster bows away from the bridge. In this exercise, you need to use the entire bow for each note value (use the bow from frog to tip; see Figure 7.15). To be successful, you will need to begin with your bow in bowing lane 3 for the quarter notes, bowing lane 2 for the half notes, and bowing lane 1 for the whole notes. Maintain a *mezzo forte* dynamic for the duration of the exercise.

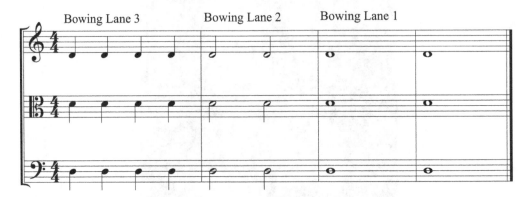

Figure 7.15 Exercise to Practice Changing Bowing Lanes

This exercise allows you to feel how the slow bow is much more easily maintained closer to the bridge. Try playing one slow long bow over the fingerboard. How many seconds can you play and maintain a good tone using only one bow? Now try playing a slow

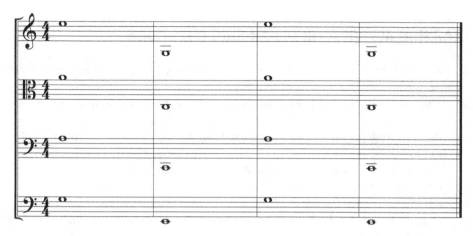

Figure 7.16 Adjust the Contact Point Closer to the Bridge on High Strings and Away From the Bridge on Lower Strings

long bow near the bridge. How many seconds can you maintain a good tone using only one bow near the bridge?

Principle 3: Move the bow closer to the bridge when playing on higher strings and away from the bridge when playing on lower strings. Try using bowing lane 1 for your highest string and bowing lane 3 for your lowest string. The bowing lanes are not exact, but you will find that it is easier to get a good sound on the lower strings if you adjust your contact point farther away from the bridge than you would for your highest string.

Principle 4: Move the bow closer to the bridge to play in higher positions (see Figure 7.17). This is the same concept as Principle 3. When players shift into higher positions, the string is shortened, which also changes the most resonant point on the string. The higher the position, the closer the player should move to the bridge. Try playing open A; then find the A that is one octave higher (stay on the A string). You will find that you need to move your bow toward the bridge, or you may even hit the other strings.

Figure 7.17 Adjust the Contact Point Closer to the Bridge in High Positions and Away from the Bridge in Lower Positions

LEARNING ACTIVITY 7B: DISCUSSION QUESTIONS

1.   What are three possible reasons that a student may be performing with an airy sound?
2.   What are three possible reasons that a student may be performing with a choked sound?
3.   Should a student move towards or away from the bridge when playing in higher positions?
4.   Why are bass bows shorter and heavier than violin bows?
5.   What does *bow distribution* mean?
6.   What does *bow placement* mean?
7.   Why should initial rhythms be introduced in even bowing patterns when first teaching students to bow?
8.   Should slow bows be performed close to or away from the bridge?

NOTES

1.   Rossing, T. D. & Hanson, R. J. (2010). *Bowed strings: Chapter in the science of string instruments*. T. D. Rossing (Ed.), p. 197; Howard, D. & Angus, J. (2017). *Acoustics and psychoacoustics* (5th ed.). New York, NY: Routledge.
2.   Rolland, P., Mutschler, M. & Hellebrandt, F. A. (2000). *The teaching of action in string playing: Developmental and remedial techniques [for] violin and viola*. Urbana, IL: Illinois String Research Associates, p. 165.
3.   Erdlee, E. (1988). *The mastery of the bow*; Potter, L. Tamarac, Fla.: Distinctive Pub; Potter, L. (1973). *The Art of cello playing*. (revised ed.), Evanston, Ill: Summy-Birchard Co, p. 23.
4.   Stoeving, P. (1920). *The mastery of the bow and bowing subtleties*. New York, NY: Carl Fischer, Inc. Simandl, F. (1984). *New method for the double bass*. Book 1. Revised by Zimmerman. New York: Carl Fischer, Inc, p. 5.
5.   Fischer, S. (2012). *Tone: Experimenting with proportions on the violin*. London: Fitzroy Music Press.
6.   Rolland, P. (2000), p. 165.
7.   Fischer, S. (2012), p. vii.
8.   Roederer, J. G. (2008). *The physics and psychophysics of music: An introduction*. New York, NY: Springer, p. 125.
9.   Backus, J. (1977). *The acoustical foundations of music*. New York: Norton & Company.
10. Fletcher, N. H. & Rossing, T. D. (1991). *The physics of musical instruments*. New York, NY: Springer-Verlag.
11. Galamian, I. (1985). *Principles of violin playing & teaching*. Englewood Cliffs, NJ: Prentice-Hall.
12. MENC Task Force on String Education Course of Study. (1991). *Teaching stringed instruments: A course of study*. Reston, VA: Music Educators National Conference.
13. Flesch, C. & Saenger, G. (1934). *Problems of tone production in violin playing*. New York, NY: Carl Fischer, Inc.
14. Fischer, S. & Edition Peters. (1997). *Basics: 300 exercises and practice routines for the violin*. London: Edition Peters, p. 41.

CHAPTER 8

Basic Articulations

String players have a wide range of articulations that they are able to execute. *Guide to Orchestral Bowing Through Musical Styles* by Marvin Rabin and Priscilla Smith describes and provides video examples of 30 different articulations commonly used by string players to perform orchestral repertoire.[1] There are many excellent online resources that describe the various articulations in-depth such as the String Pedagogy Notebook (http://stringtechnique.com/), violinmaster-class.com, and violinonline.com. The purpose of this chapter is to provide an overview of the 10 most basic and essential articulations used in beginning and intermediate string playing: pizzicato, detaché, collé, martelé, legato, slurs, hooked bows, and three foundational off-the-string strokes: brush stroke, spiccato, and sautillé. For more detailed descriptions and a more thorough list, explore the list of additional resources included at the end of the chapter.

PIZZICATO

Pizzicato is frequently the first articulation introduced to beginning players in group string classes and can be executed without the bow or while holding the bow.

Pizzicato Without the Bow

Plucking the string without the bow is introduced early and is usually performed with the index finger, but there are some exceptions. For instance, violin and viola players use their thumb when plucking in guitar position, and bass players will sometimes alternate between using first and second finger to pluck the string, thereby minimizing the potential of developing a blister. Violin and viola players should the fleshy portion of their fingertip when plucking and gently pull and release the string diagonally. Cello players will use more of the flesh of the fingertip to get a richer tone. Bass players generally pluck more horizontally using the side of the finger from the tip to the first knuckle.

The best location to pluck the string on each instrument is at the most resonant point over the fingerboard, not in the bowing lane. A good starting point is a few inches from the end of the fingerboard. Do not be tempted to have students' anchor their thumbs under the corner of the fingerboard. As players advance, the contact point of the pizzicato should be moveable. The most resonant place on the string will move closer to the bridge when students shift their left hand to play higher notes because the string is shortened. Generally speaking, players should pluck farther away from the bridge when in first position and closer to the bridge when playing in higher positions. For this reason, have students place their thumb along the side of the fingerboard when plucking.

Pizzicato With the Bow

Players will need to perform arco (with the bow), then quickly transition to pizzicato (plucking), and the reverse. Students need to learn how to hold the bow as they pluck, as well as how to transition from bow hold to pizzicato then back to bow hold. When performing pizzicato with the bow in the right hand, the frog of the bow is held by fingers 2, 3, and 4 so that the thumb and index finger are free to pluck the string. Students should make a bow hold, then pull the bow into the palm of the hand to free the thumb and index finger for pizzicato (see Figure 8.1). The process for German bass bow is slightly different. The frog of the bow is already near the palm of the hand. The student will pull the bow into the hand and fingers 2, 3, and 4 will support the bow with the tip facing the floor. The thumb and index finger will then be free to pluck the string (see Figure 8.1).

Figure 8.1 Pizzicato With the Bow

DETACHÉ

Detaché directly translated means detached, which should not be confused with staccato or short note lengths. "The goal of detaché is evenness of tone and connection between notes"[2] (Green, p. 70). Smooth bow direction changes are an important aspect of the detaché bow stroke. To execute a bow change smoothly, the player's fingers and wrist must be flexible. Creating even speed and weight during the bow change and feeling as though the bow is "magnetized" to the string throughout the direction change allows the sound to remain continuous. One variation of the detaché bow stroke includes a slightly more articulate stroke where the bow direction change makes a clicking sound. This variation on the bow stroke is popular and provides a gateway to martelé and other more articulated bow strokes.[3]

String Crossings

While students are learning to perform detaché, they must also negotiate string crossings. To understand string crossings, the teacher must first become aware of how the instrument is oriented from the lowest pitched string to highest pitched string in relation to the students' bodies. Consider the fact that violinists and violists are looking towards their fingerboard, while cellists and bassists are facing their bridges. Because of this orientation, violinists and violists need to *raise* their right elbow to perform their lowest pitched string (G and C), while cellist and bassists need to *lower* their right elbow in order to play their lowest strings (C and E). In this section of the text "lower string" will refer to the physically lower string in the following explanations rather than to the pitch of the string.

For beginner and intermediate players, there are two types of string crossings:

1. Level Changes—

This is the most basic string crossing that requires the elbow height of the bow arm to change to accommodate the string on which the pitches will be performed. There are seven different levels of the bow when crossing strings[4]—the level for each string and the level in between two strings that allows a double stop to be performed. Simon Fisher (2012) identifies the seven levels as follows: L1—G string, L2—G/D double stop, L3—D string, L4—D/A double stop, L5—A string, L6—A/E double stop, and L7—E string (p. 25).[5] Level changes are used to perform passages that remain on one string for a succession of notes. The first phrase of *Twinkle Twinkle Little Star* is a good example of a basic level change (see Figure 8.2).

To perform this passage, violin and viola players will lower their right elbow to access the A string comfortably; cello and bass players will raise the right elbow to access the A string or G string, in the case of the bassist.

2. Rapid String Crossings—

When a passage requires that players alternate rapidly between two strings, the string crossing is performed with the wrist and forearm while the elbow remains at the height of the lower string (physically lower, not necessarily lower in pitch). During these passages, string players will either use a counter clockwise motion with the wrist and forearm (see

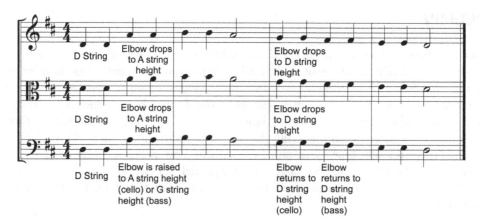

Figure 8.2 Bow Level Change

Figure 8.3 Rapid String Crossings Using a Counter Clockwise Motion

Figure 8.4 Rapid String Crossings Counter Clockwise

Figure 8.3) or a clockwise motion (see Figure 8.4) depending on whether they are changing from a lower string to a higher string (clockwise) or higher string to a lower string (counterclockwise). In Figure 8.3, the elbow remains at the E string height while the wrist and forearm execute the string crossing using a counterclockwise motion. (This is from the player's perspective. In Video 8.4a you will view this from a teacher's perspective, in which case the motion will appear clockwise).

Rapid string crossings are executed similarly across the four bowed string instruments, but because of the orientation of the instrument, it may seem opposite. In Figure 8.5, violinists would use a counterclockwise motion, and the cellists and bassists would use a clockwise motion.

There are exceptions to these rules. Sometimes, when a passage includes rapid string crossings and repeated notes on a string, the player will generally choose an elbow height that accommodates the string level on which the majority of the notes occur. The opening violin 1 part of Handel's *Entrance of the Queen of Sheba* is a good example (Figure 8.6, Video 8.5).

As a general rule, string crossings at faster speeds are more easily executed in the middle of the bow.[6] This is because the physical distance that the hand and elbow need travel is reduced as the bow placement approaches the frog. Maintaining contact with the string, as though the bow were adhered to the string, facilitates a quality tone and smooth string crossing.

Figure 8.5 Rapid String Crossings for High and Low Strings

Figure 8.6 Violin 1 Excerpt from Handel's Entrance of the Queen of Sheba

COLLÉ

8.6a

8.6b

8.6c

The collé bow stroke is an important technique for beginning string players because it forms the foundation for a number of other bow strokes, such as martelé, marcato, and staccato. The French translation of *collé* is "glued." The bow grabs the string so that the very first sound is clear and articulate. Have students silently "wiggle" their string back and forth, then rapidly release the weight, and pull the bow immediately off the string as if the bow were performing pizzicato. The results sound should be clear, short, and resonant. Make sure that students are able to execute this stroke using primary their wrist and fingers.

MARTELÉ

8.7a

8.7b

8.7c

The martelé bow stroke utilizes a similar attack as the collé stroke, but rather than coming off the string to release the sound, the bow remains on the string. There are three parts to this bow stroke: the initial attack when the bow "grips" the string, a fast bow speed that sustains the note for approximately half of its notated duration,[7] and the end of the stroke when the bow remains on the string during the pause between notes.[8] Stopping the bow without choking the sound can be difficult for beginners. Students must learn to start the sound with a "sticky" bow, pull the bow quickly to generate resonance, and then stop the bow releasing all weight. This stroke can be performed in any portion of the bow but is more often performed in the middle to upper half. The martelé bow stroke may be notated with a dot, a hammer-head, or accents or have no indication. Teachers and students should investigate the performance practice and traditions of a given piece of music to determine the correct articulation.

LEGATO AND SLURS

8.8a

8.8b

Legato strokes include both slurred notes, where multiple pitches are played in one bow, or connected detaché in which the bow changes are barely evident. Consistent bow speed, consistent bow weight, and flexibility are essential to legato bow changes. The sound produced by the bow during the change must be as seamless as possible. Galamian (1962) succinctly described a fluid bow change as follows:

> Some methods prescribe the use of fingers alone, other the hand and wrist, still others the forearm or whole arm. Yet the essence of the matter does *not* lie in the particular muscles or joints that should participate, but instead in two factors: (1) the bow has to slow down shortly before the change, and (2) the pressure has to be lightened, with both of these elements delicately and precisely coordinated.
>
> (p. 86)

Students should strive for a constant sound and avoid stopping or speeding up the bow during bow changes.

HOOKED AND LINKED BOWS

8.9a ▶ Hooked and linked bows are not articulations but, rather, are bowing techniques that are introduced immediately before or after teaching slurs. Linked bows allow students to perform two
8.9b ▶ separate notes of even value using the same bow direction.[9] The linked bow can be performed legato or separated depending on the style of the piece. Young players need to gain the control necessary to stop and restart the bow again in the same direction (see Video 8.8a). The opening of Minuet No. 1 by Bach in Suzuki Book I is an example of a linked bow (see Figure 8.7).[10]

Hooked bows are similar to linked bows but are used for notes uneven in length. Uneven patterns such as dotted-eight–sixteenth-note patterns and quarter- and eighth-note patterns[11] (see Figure 8.8).

Figure 8.7 Notation of Linked Bow Stroke

Figure 8.8 Notation of Hooked Bow Stroke

8.10a ▶ ## OFF-THE-STRING STROKES

8.10b ▶ ### Spiccato

8.10c ▶ Spiccato can be classified into two general categories for the beginner to intermediate player: brush stroke or spiccato.[12] The brush stroke is used in slower tempi, occurs nearer to the frog, and uses primarily horizontal motion to create broad off-the-string strokes. Spiccato is technically a stroke that begins off the string and rebounds back off the string.[13] This stroke occurs at a faster tempo than the brush stroke and is performed near the balance point. Rolland (2010) recommends having students return to the beginning bow hold (holding the bow at the balance point) when first attempting this articulation.[14] By holding the bow at the balance point, the bow feels lighter, and students have more control over their first attempts at bouncing. Combining this strategy with holding the bow at the frog and exploring the natural bounce of one's bow without horizontal motion, is a good way to introduce spiccato. Off-the-string strokes are generally indicated with a dot, similar to martelé. Again, teachers and students are responsible for researching the performance practice of a given piece or period to determine the correct bow stroke.

Sautillé

The sautillé bow stroke is a very fast off-the-string stroke that begins on the string and barely leaves the string. "In sautillé the wood of the bow bounces without the hair leaving the string (although at times it can). It has to be played in a particular place on the bow, usually somewhere around the middle, where the stick has the greatest natural bounce" (Fischer, 2012, p. 73). Sautillé is performed between the balance point and middle of the bow and is generally employed at tempi around and faster than a quarter note at 150.

When bouncing the bow, as a general rule, slower tempi are performed closer to the frog, and faster tempi are performed closer to the middle. Every bow is different, and students will need to explore bouncing at different tempi in different parts of the bow to discover the best location for each stroke.

LEARNING ACTIVITY 8: INTERVIEW A STRING PLAYER

There numerous philosophies regarding the mechanics of the bow arm, particularly pertaining to the execution of various articulations. Talking with string players about how to execute different articulations can be very enlightening. New teachers should find out what others think about the way different articulations are executed by the bow arm. Interview some string players and teachers to find out their views on the following:

1. How do you play martelé? How do you know when to use this type of bow stroke?
2. What does marcato mean? How do you know when to use a marcato bow stroke?
3. Does spiccato start on or off the string?
4. When you use spiccato, do you use a flat or rotated bow hair?
5. How do you get the bow to bounce?
6. Can you explain the difference between a brush stroke, spiccato stroke, and sautillé stroke?

Do not be surprised if you get different responses from different players. Compare the different responses in a class discussion.

NOTES

1.   Rabin, M. & Smith, P. (1990). *Guide to orchestral bowings through musical styles*. Madison, WI: University of Wisconsin-Madison, Really Good Music, LLC.
2.   Green, E. A. H. (1999). *Teaching stringed instruments in classes*. Fairfax, VA: American String Teachers Association.
3.   Sassmannshaus, K. (2012). *Violinmasterclass.com*. Starling Project Foundation, Inc. Retrieved from www.violinmasterclass.com/en/masterclasses/right-hand/detache.
4.   Stoeving, P. (1931). *The master of the bow and bowing subtleties*. New York, NY: Carl Fischer, Inc.
5.   Fischer, S. (2012). *Basics: 300 exercises and practice routines for the violin*. London: Peters Edition Limited.
6.   Kjelland, J. (2003). *Orchestral bowing: Style and function*. Van Nuys, CA: Alfred Music.
7.   Stoeving, P. (1931).
8.   Galamian, I. (1963). *Principles of violin playing and teaching*. (2nd ed.). Englewood Cliffs, NJ: Prentice Hall.
9.   Rabin, M. & Smith, P. (1984). *Guide to orchestral bowings through musical styles*. Madison, WI: University of Wisconsin Extension—Arts.
10. Suzuki, S. (2018). *Suzuki violin school*. (Rev. ed., Vol. I). Van Nuys, CA: Alfred Music.
11. Rabin, M. & Smith, P. (1984).
12. Kjelland, J. (2003).
13. Green, E. A. H. (1999); Fischer, S. (2012); Galamian, I. (1962); Kjelland, J. (2003).
14. Rolland, P., Mutchler, M. & Hellebrandt, F. (2010). *The teaching of action in string playing*. (3rd ed.). Urbana, IL: Illinois String Research Associates.

CHAPTER 9

Bowing Guidelines

Orchestras strive to have uniformity with their bow strokes within a section (e.g. violin 1, violin 2, etc.). This uniformity includes using the same bow direction and bow-placement as the principal player. To do this, bowings must be determined by the conductor, concertmaster, or, in the case of the school orchestra, the teacher. The purpose of this chapter is to simplify what is a very complex topic. String players rarely agree on bowings, and the same piece can be played successfully with a variety of bowings. So how does one determine in which direction the bow should go? Probably the most important guiding principle is to choose the easiest bowing that will allow the players to achieve the intended musical result.[1]

There are some excellent resources that elaborate on the topic of bowings, such as *Orchestral Bowings and Routines* by Elizabeth A. H. Green,[2] *Orchestral Bowing: Style and Function* by James Kjelland,[3] *Guide to Orchestral Bowings Through Musical Styles* by Marvin Rabin,[4] and *Manual of Orchestra Bowing* by Charles Gigante.[5] These resources are invaluable in determining which direction the bow should go.

A number of musical variables have an impact on bowing choices. Style and articulation, rhythm, bow placement, bow distribution, musical phrasing, and dynamics must all be considered. The same passage performed legato and then staccato may require a different bowing. Similarly, dynamics or accents require a different approach. When choosing bowings, consider the following guidelines. None of these rules will apply in all situations, and there is usually more than one correct way to bow any given passage.

PRINCIPLE 1: *PLAY DOWN-BOW ON THE DOWNBEATS AND UP-BOW ON THE UPBEATS*

This is the most basic of the rules that string players follow. Because the frog of the bow is heavier and the tip lighter, aligning the natural weight of the bow with the strong beats is more natural. If a given passage allows the players to play down-bow on the strong beats and up-bow on the upbeats, string players will play the passage, "as it comes," which means that they will not alter the bow directions. There is an exception to this rule called the law of compensation. "The Law of Compensation states that if the bowing naturally readjusts itself in the space of two measures, the player need not change it in any way"[6] (p. 12, Green, 2010).

Sometimes string players need to adjust the bowings so that the downbeat can be played with a down-bow. There are four solutions that a player may choose: (a) retake the bow, (b) add a double up-bow, (c) play a double down-bow, or (d) add a slur.

Retake

Retakes, or playing down-bow, then lifting, and placing the bow back at the frog to play another down-bow, are most frequently used when there are rests that allow ample time for the bow to be lifted and placed again onto the string (see Figure 9.1). Retakes are also used at the end of a phrase where a natural breath would occur between the phrases in the music.

Figure 9.1 Excerpt from Vivaldi's *Concerto in A Minor for Two Violins*

Add an Up-Bow

When a downbeat does not naturally arrive on a down-bow, string players will often add an up-bow somewhere in the measure. Usually, string players will choose to hook the bow so that the bow distribution logically allows them to return to a specific location in the bow. For example, in Figure 9.2, string players would likely choose to hook the eighth notes so that both measures were performed with a consistent articulation.

You will also find passages that are easier to play musically when an up-bow is added on the note prior to the downbeat (see Figure 9.3).

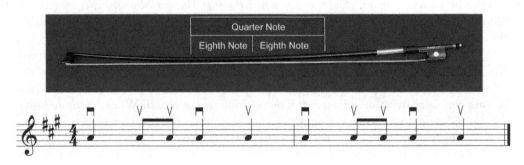

Figure 9.2 Add an Up-bow

Figure 9.3 Passage from "Farandole," *L'Arlessiene Suite* by Bizet

Double Down-Bow

Like double up-bows, double down-bows are also used to even out bow distribution when note values are uneven or during more rapid passages that have an eighth note followed by two sixteenth notes and the eighth note can be played short (see Figure 9.4).

Figure 9.4 Passage from *Capriccio Espagnol* by Rimsky-Korsakov

Add or Remove a Slur

Sometimes it is helpful to add a slur when stylistically appropriate. Slurs may be added or removed to allow for more practical bowings. The second violin part of the "Sarabande" in the Holberg's *Suite for Strings* is an example of a passage that can be bowed a number of ways by eliminating or adding slurs (see Figure 9.5).

Figure 9.5 II. "Sarabande" from the Holberg's *Suite for Strings*

The passage may be performed by a professional group as written. Some groups may choose to change the bowings for additional control. For example, a younger group may want to avoid performing a string crossing during a slur, so the players may choose to rebow the third measure as follows (see Figure 9.6). Likewise, it may be difficult to end the phrase on an up-bow, so the two sixteenth notes in bar 4 may be slurred together.

Figure 9.6 Adding Slurs to Increase Bow Control

PRINCIPLE 2: *UP-BOW TO CRESCENDO AND DOWN-BOW TO DECRESCENDO*

Like Principle 1, the natural weight of the bow at the frog has an impact on bowing choices because it is generally easier to play louder at the frog and softer at the tip. String players prefer to perform crescendos up-bow and decrescendos down-bow when possible. Again, Holberg's *Suite for Strings*, movement 2, second violin part provides an example of a passage that string players may prefer to bow differently to achieve the desired musical result (see Figure 9.7).

Figure 9.7 Second Violin Part of "Sarabande" from Holberg's *Suite for Strings*

Beginning the passage on an up-bow may actually be preferred by some players because the first crescendo will then arrive on an up-bow. The performers may choose to break apart the bowing in the second phrase so that the decrescendo can be performed down-bow.

PRINCIPLE 3: *THE EVEN/ODD RULE*

The even/odd rule explains how to approach entrances following rests or pickups at the beginning of a piece. When there are an even number of bowings preceding the downbeat, these should begin down-bow; when there are an odd number of bowings preceding the downbeat, these should begin up-bow. In many ways, this is simply another way to achieve the first bowing rule and consistently arrive down-bow on the downbeat. Be careful to notice that it is an even or odd number of *bowings*, not the number of notes, that should be taken into account. Many viola and cello parts illustrate this principle effectively. See Figure 9.8.

Figure 9.8 Place an Up-bow on an Odd Number of Bowings so that the Downbeat Can Be Performed with a Down-bow. Likewise, Place a Down-bow When There Are an Even Number of Bowings Prior to the Downbeat.

PRINCIPLE 4: *UNEVEN RHYTHM PATTERNS ARE OFTEN HOOKED OR LINKED*

Uneven rhythmic figures such as dotted–eighth–sixteenth notes and triple meter patterns that repeatedly play a quarter followed by eighth note are generally performed hooked or linked (see Figure 9.9). By performing these patterns using the same bow, direction players have more control because the bow is distributed evenly.

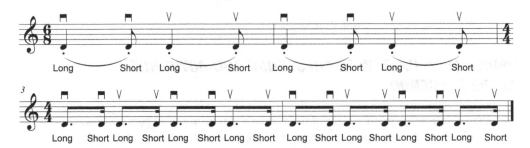

Figure 9.9 Hooked and Linked Bowings

Stopping the bow and rearticulating the sixteenth note allows the sixteenth to be crisper, and the player is able to return to the place in the bow where they began the bow stroke.

"Farandole" from L'Arlessienne Suite No. 2 by Bizet contains dotted rhythm patterns that can be performed hooked so that the player repeatedly returns to the balance point of the bow (see Figure 9.10).

Figure 9.10 "Farandole" from the *L'Arlessiene Suite* by Bizet

Hooked bows can be indicated two different ways (see Figure 9.9). A tie with a dot indicates to a string player that the bow should stop and restart in the same direction. Similarly, placing the bow directions above the notes will also communicate to a string player that the bow should stop and restart in the same direction.

GENERAL CONSIDERATIONS

Choosing good bowings takes practice and experience. Bowings should be prepared prior to rehearsing and should be marked in both score and parts. Bowings are placed above the notes, with the exception of divisi sections, in which case the lower divisi bowings may be indicated beneath the notes. Sometimes the most practical bowing is not the same for low strings and high strings, so it is acceptable for the same passage to be performed differently by two sections of the orchestra.

LEARNING ACTIVITY 9: PRACTICE CHOOSING BOWINGS

"Silvie" is a song that can be performed with a number of different bowings. Try bowing this simple arrangement (see Figure 9.11) following the basic bowing principles outlined in this chapter. Discuss your bowing solutions in class.

1. Where might it be appropriate to add a retake so that the downbeat of the second phrase can be performed down-bow?
2. Choose a different solution: rather than using a retake try adding some slurs to make the bowing more musical.
3. Choose yet another solution that will allow for the most even bow distribution. You can choose to retake, add slurs, or use hooked bows.
4. What rule applies to the second part in the second measure following rests?

Figure 9.11 Practice Different Bowings

NOTES

1.   Kjelland, J. (2003). *Orchestral bowing: Style and function.* Van Nuys, CA: Alfred Music.
2.   Green, E. A. H. (2010). *Orchestral bowings and routines.* Fairfax, VA: American String Teachers Association with National School Orchestra Association.
3.   Kjelland, J. (2003).
4.   Rabin, M. & Smith, P. (1984). *Guide to orchestral bowings through musical styles.* Madison, WI: University of Wisconsin Extension—Arts.
5.   Gigante, C. (1986). *Manual of orchestral bowing.* Bryn Mawr, PA: American String Teachers Association.
6.   Green, E. A. H. (2010).

PART II

Understanding Fingerings
Patterns and Positions

Perhaps one of the most mysterious aspects of teaching a string instrument is how to determine the best fingering to use. String fingerings can be confusing to non-native string players because any given note has a minimum of 16 different possibilities in terms of which finger, string, and position is used. Choosing a good fingering is a bit like trying to solve an equation or choosing which road to use when trying to go from point A to point B. There is usually more than one road that you can take to get to a destination. Sometimes you choose the most efficient path, while other times a more scenic route may be preferred. Good fingers are logical and help the player achieve the desired musical results. The three fingering chapters included in this text are designed to provide string teachers with the necessary tools to understand the finger patterns used for each of the instruments, fingerboard geography (or physical location of the pitches along the fingerboard), and how to combine finger patterns and positions to create logical fingerings.

COMMONALITIES AMONG THE FOUR BOWED INSTRUMENTS

Instrument Ranges

The violin and viola share a similar range. The A string of both the violin and viola is typically tuned to A 440 Hz. The A, D, and G string all sound in the same range. The viola can play a fifth lower with the addition of the C string, and the violin is able to play higher

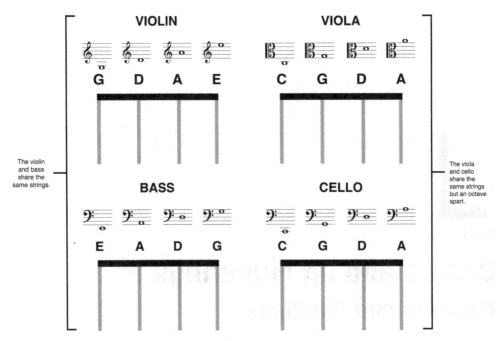

Figure X.1 The Open Strings of the Violin, Viola, Cello, and Bass

because of the E string. The cello A sounds an octave lower (220 Hz) than the violin and viola. The viola and cello share the same strings separated by an octave. The double bass is actually a transposing instrument. The A string is tuned two octaves lower than the cello (55 Hz). The double bass and violin share the same strings (E, A, D, G) but in reverse order because the violin is tuned in fifths and the bass in fourths. Strings A, D, and G are in common between the four instruments. Review where the open strings are notated on the music staff (see Figure X.1).

FINGERBOARD GEOGRAPHY

Fingerboard geography refers to the locations of pitches along the fingerboard. The fingerboard geography for all string instruments is essentially the same. Each of the strings can be evenly divided by half step. The example below shows the G string with each ascending half step labeled.

Beginning with the open strings, ascending half steps can be identified on each string to construct the fingerboard geography. When looking at the fingerboard geography charts (Figure X.2), one can see that the fingerboard map for each string is the same regardless of instrument. It is the fingering patterns required to play each instrument that changes to accommodate the different sizes of each instrument in relation to the hand.

THE POSITIONS

Various labeling systems have been used to organize the positions on bowed string instruments. The most commonly used position systems for heterogeneous instruction are

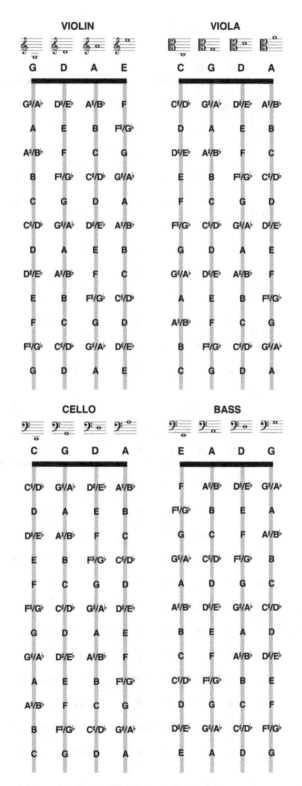

Figure X.2 Fingerboard Maps for the Violin, Viola, Cello, and Bass

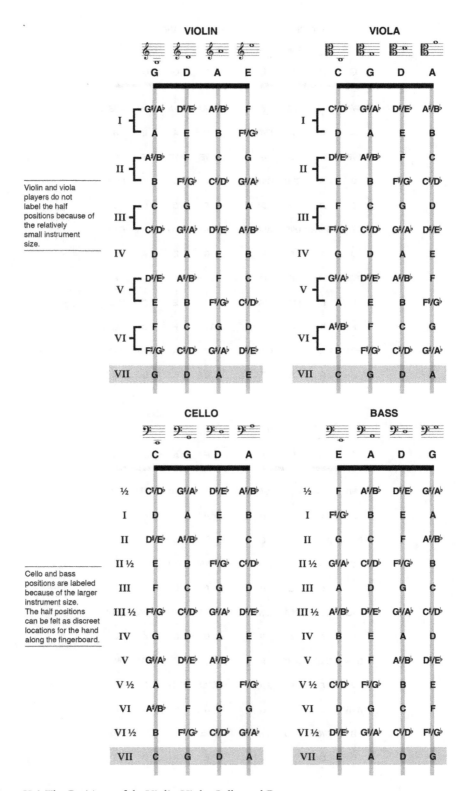

Figure X.3 The Positions of the Violin, Viola, Cello, and Bass

illustrated in Figure X.3. You can see that the cello and bass systems label half positions, violin, and viola label only the whole positions.

Seventh position (VII) is an octave higher than the open string. This position also coincides with the halfway harmonic, or the location where the string is divided in half. Natural harmonics on a string instrument occur at the ½, ⅓ and ¼ of each string. By lightly touching (not compressing) the string, the harmonic is produced. Seventh position is also the location where thumb position begins on both cello and bass.

SHIFTING

String players shift, or move the location of their hand into various positions for the following reasons: to reach higher pitches, to maximize notes in a single position, to avoid strings crossings, to avoid open strings (add vibrato, adjust pitch, or darken tone quality), to change the tone color of the sound (lower strings in higher positions provide a darker tone than lower positions on higher strings), or to add expressive elements such as portamento (or an audible and expressive shift). Shifting requires proper instrument position, flexibility, and a relaxed left hand.

The concepts for fingerings apply consistently across the four instruments. The following chapters sequentially explain finger patterns, positions, and fingering guidelines for violin, viola, cello, and bass. Each concept is accompanied by an interactive online tutorial. The tutorials interface with mobile devices and smart boards. The author recommends completing the tutorial and submitting a screenshot of the final frame to your instructor.

CHAPTER 10

Violin and Viola Fingerings

The violin and viola share similar technique. Because the two instruments are similar, most right- and left-hand concepts transfer from one instrument to the other. When teaching in a heterogeneous setting, delivering instruction to the violin and viola players simultaneously is advantageous and promotes efficient pacing. For this reason, the beginning of this chapter focuses on the left-hand concepts that apply to both instruments. These concepts include (a) four basic diatonic finger patterns, (b) fingerboard geography (the location of the pitches on the fingerboard), (c) the positions, and (d) guidelines for choosing basic fingerings for the beginning violin or viola player.

THE FOUR BASIC FINGER PATTERNS

The musical distance between each finger on the violin or viola is generally a half step or whole step depending on the spacing of the fingers. On occasion, violin and viola players may stretch to accommodate up to a minor third between fingers. In general, the fingers are either placed next to one another (touching or nearly touching) to produce a half step or with a space between the fingers to produce a whole step (Figure 10.1). Using the typical hand frame, the violinist or violist can easily perform a perfect fourth from fingers 1 to 4.

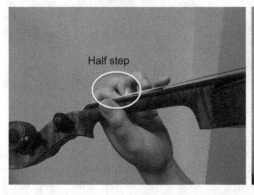 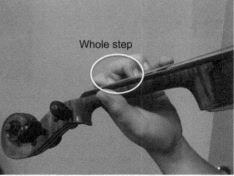

Figure 10.1 An Example of Finger Placement for Half Steps and Whole Steps

There are four diatonic finger patterns that violin and viola players use most frequently. Each finger pattern is named after the location of the half step between fingers.[1],[2] Bornoff originally conceived of five finger patterns that were taught sequentially to promote proper left-hand shape during small group or individual instruction. The Bornoff finger patterns provide the conceptual framework for this chapter. These patterns have been reduced to four and reordered to adapt instruction for a heterogeneously grouped class.

1. **Finger Pattern 1** (see Figure 10.2) is referred to as the 2–3 finger pattern because the half step occurs between fingers 2 and 3 allowing the player to perform whole step, half step, whole step.

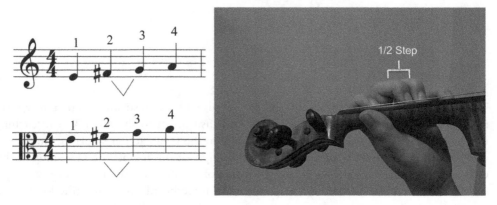

Figure 10.2 Finger Pattern 1—The Half Step Falls Between Fingers 2 and 3

2. **Finger Pattern 2** (see Figure 10.3) is called the 1–2 finger pattern because the half step falls between fingers 1 and 2 allowing the player to perform half step, whole step, whole step when ascending or whole step, whole step, half step when descending.

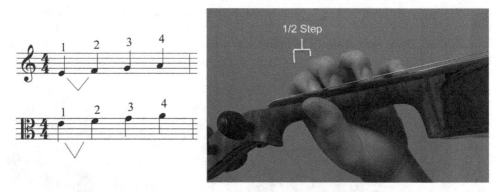

Figure 10.3 Finger Pattern 2—The Half Step Falls Between Fingers 1 and 2

3. **Finger Pattern 3** (see Figure 10.4) is called the 3–4 finger pattern because the half step naturally falls between fingers 3 and 4. This finger pattern allows the player to perform whole step, whole step, half step when ascending or half step, whole step, whole step when descending.

Figure 10.4 Finger Pattern 3—the Half Step Falls Between Fingers 3 and 4

4. **Finger Pattern 4** (see Figure 10.5) is named the open finger pattern because this pattern allows the player to perform three consecutive whole steps and none of the fingers touch.

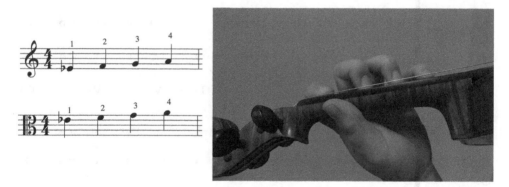

Figure 10.5 Finger Pattern 4—Three Consecutive Whole Steps.

These four finger patterns can be played in any position on the instrument. Practice applying these four basic finger patterns in first position.

LEARNING ACTIVITY 10A (ONLINE TUTORIAL 1: PRACTICE VIOLIN AND VIOLA FINGER PATTERNS)

Practice selecting violin and viola finger patterns. Send a screenshot of the final frame to your teacher.

Link to violin tutorial 1—http://teachingstrings.online/tutorials/violin/Violin Tutorial1/

Link to viola tutorial 1—http://teachingstrings.online/tutorials/viola/ViolaTu torial1/

FINGERBOARD GEOGRAPHY

Fingerboard geography on all four bowed string instruments is essentially the same. The fingerboard can be divided into half steps, with each half step representing a new position. While cello and bass use positions ½, I, II, II ½, III, III ½, and so on (see Chapters 11 and 12), violin and viola methods do not recognize the half positions as discreet positions. Rather, the positions used to organize the violin and viola fingerboard include I, II, III, IV, V, VI, and VII. In theory, the half positions exist, but most violin and viola systems do not label these positions. Because the instrument is smaller, the physical distance between notes on the fingerboard is smaller, so it is easier to conceive of the positions as whole positions rather than accounting for every half step.

The open strings of the violin, viola, and cello are tuned in fifths. The open strings of the violin include G, D, A, and E, and the open strings of the viola include C, G, D, and A (see Figure 10.6).

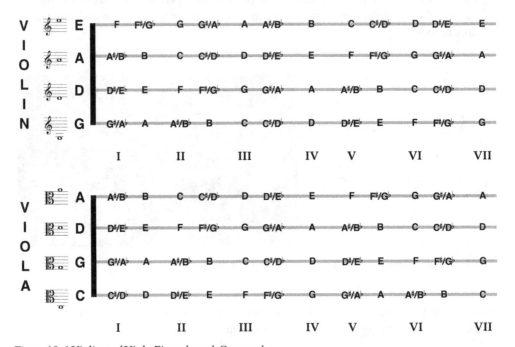

Figure 10.6 Violin and Viola Fingerboard Geography

Like the cello and bass, seventh position (VII) is an octave higher than the open string. This position also coincides with the halfway harmonic, or the location where the string is divided in half. Natural harmonics on a string instrument occur at the ½, ⅓ and ¼ of each string. By lightly touching (not compressing) the string, the harmonic is produced.

THE POSITIONS

In most instances, the location of the player's first finger determines the position in which the violinist or violist is considered to be playing. For example, if the player's first finger falls on the note E or E♭ on the D string, then the player is in first position (I) and is able to perform the highlighted notes below across the four strings without shifting (see Figure 10.7).

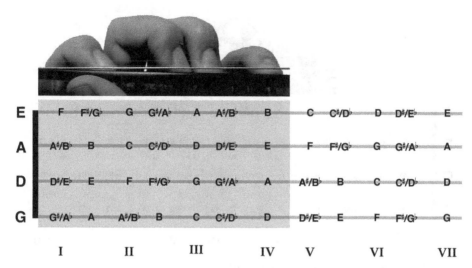

Figure 10.7 First Position on the Violin (position I)

Therefore, if the violinist or violists' first finger falls on the note F on the D string, then the player is in second position (II) and is able to perform the following notes across the four strings (see Figure 10.8).

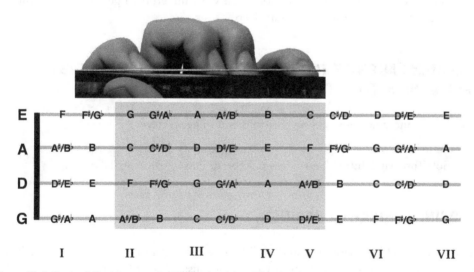

Figure 10.8 Second Position on the Violin (position II)

To further illustrate this concept, imagine that a violist has her fourth finger on the pitch G on the A string. On what note would the first finger fall? If you look at Figure 10.9, you will see that the first finger falls on the D, which is located in third position (III).

If a player's first finger falls on C#/D♭ on the A string or F#/G♭ on the D string, whether the player is technically in second or third position is a matter of debate. As a general rule, if the player is playing C# or F#, the player will likely associate those pitches with second position, while D♭ and G♭ will be associated with third position. When in first position, violinists, and violists have the ability to reach the first finger back a half step to

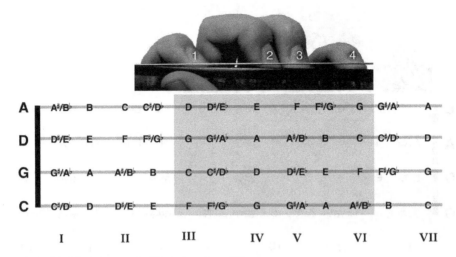

Figure 10.9 Third Position on the Viola (position III)

play the half step above the open string. String players refer to this as using "low one" and sometimes prefer this approach to shifting. Practically speaking, it does not matter whether the player conceives of second position, third position, or even "second and a half position" as long as the left hand is able to play the pitches in tune. For the purpose of providing a clear framework for understanding violin and viola fingerboard geography, this tutorial labels the positions as indicated in Figure 10.6.

LEARNING ACTIVITY 10B (ONLINE TUTORIAL 2: COMBINING PATTERNS AND POSITIONS)

Go online and practice selecting positions and finger patterns.

Violin Tutorial 2: http://aim-ed.com/experiments/violindemo/tutorial2/
Viola Tutorial 2: http://aim-ed.com/experiments/violademo/tutorial2/

CHOOSING LOGICAL FINGERINGS

Like the cello and bass, violinists, and violists have more than one option for which fingering they may choose for any given passage of music. This is because the same pitches can be performed in more than one location on the fingerboard and with more than one finger (1, 2, 3, or 4). The guidelines for choosing logical fingerings are the same for all string instruments and include maximize notes in a single position, use near shifts, use landmark positions, avoid awkward string crossings, avoid open strings, and tempo and style affect fingering choice. The smaller physical distance between the pitches on the fingerboard of the violin and viola, however, allows violinists and violists to perform a wider range of pitches prior to shifting than their low string counterparts. The bassist's hand only spans the musical distance of one whole step in the lower positions, the cellist can accommodate up to a major third, while violin and viola players have the ability to perform an augmented fourth in one position using only one string, and up to a tenth in one position by crossing strings. The ability to play a wider range of notes in one position increases the number of logical fingering options that a player can use for any given passage. Because there are multiple fingering options for any musical passage, there is usually more than one correct fingering that a player may consider. A good fingering will accommodate the skill level and preference of the individual player. The guidelines in this chapter are focused on choosing fingerings for beginning and intermediate level players.

SIX GUIDELINES FOR VIOLIN AND VIOLA FINGERINGS

1. **Maximize the number of notes you can play in a single position.** Economy of motion is important on all stringed instruments. Choose a fingering that limits the number of shifts and maximizes the number of notes played in a single position. This concept is particularly important for less experienced players. More experienced violin and viola players may shift more frequently to shape phrases or change tone color, while less experienced players benefit from fingerings that enable them to accurately perform the pitch and rhythm contained in a passage. Figure 10.10 is an example of a fingering that maximizes the notes played in a single position.

Figure 10.10 Position III on the Violin and Viola Using the 3–4 Finger Pattern

If the same melodic pattern began on a different note, the violinist or violist could choose another position for this passage to avoid shifting (see Figure 10.11).

Figure 10.11 Position II on the Viola Using the 3–4 Finger Pattern

Violinists and violists reading this chapter may respond, "But I could simply play either of these passages in first position without shifting." That is true. First position may even be favored by less advanced players and would certainly be used in a beginning orchestra. There is usually more than one correct fingering for any musical excerpt.

2. **Near shifts are better than far shifts.** Choose positions that minimize the physical distance between pitches, but maximize the number of notes that can be played in a given position. Choosing to shift on the smallest music interval in a passage is recommended. Violin and viola players generally shift on the interval of a half step when possible. While using near positions is an important concept for all string players, shifting on smaller musical intervals may actually be more important for the violin and viola player. In Figure 10.12, the violinist or violist would shift on the half step, thus using first and third position to play the passage.

Figure 10.12 Shift on the Smallest Musical Interval

3. **Use landmark positions (positions I, III, IV, and VII).** The notes played by the first finger in these positions are often referred to as ring tones because these pitches correspond to the open strings. When these notes are played in tune, the open string vibrates sympathetically, producing overtones that "ring." Landmark positions provide stability and security for checking pitch accuracy and are used frequently when initially training students to shift. In Figure 10.13 fourth position is illustrated.

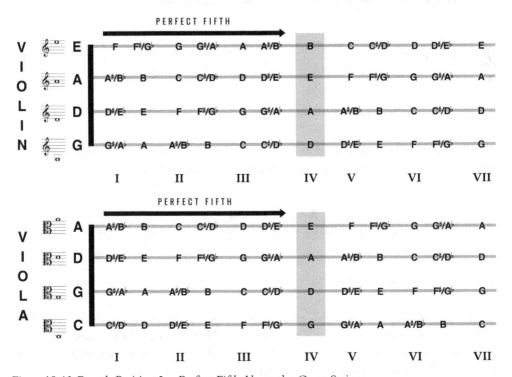

Figure 10.13 Fourth Position Is a Perfect Fifth Above the Open Strings

Because the strings on the violin and viola are tuned in fifths, the first note in fourth position on any given string is the same pitch as the higher adjacent open string. For example, in fourth position on the D string, the first finger plays the pitch A. A is a perfect fifth above D and is the same pitch as the open A string. In fourth position, players have the ability to check whether their left hand is in tune with the open strings. The security of the open string is what makes fourth position a landmark position.

Third position is also a landmark position because the first note in third position produces the identical pitch as the lower adjacent open string (see Figure 10.14). For example, the first finger in the third position on the D string is G, the same note as the open G string, only one octave higher. Third position is a perfect fourth higher than the open string on all of the string instruments.

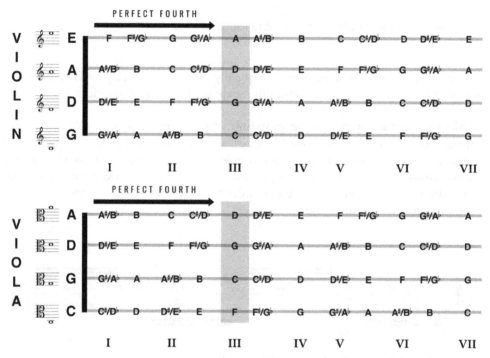

Figure 10.14 Landmark Position III

A violinist or violist may choose to use landmark positions when beginning a passage. The fingering in Figure 10.15 allows the player to use third (III) and first (I) positions. The pitch D is a ring tone. This fingering also employs using near shifts (Guideline 2).

Figure 10.15 "Ode to Joy" Using Landmark Positions

This passage could also be played in second (II) and first (I) position, but most teachers would select third (III) and first (I) position for beginning and intermediate players because those positions are landmark positions and are more familiar positions to younger players (see Figure 10.16).

Figure 10.16 "Ode to Joy" with Second (II) and First (I) Position

Landmark positions are used more frequently. However, as players become more advanced, it is important for them to become adept at playing in all positions.

4. **Shift to avoid awkward string crossings.** Passages that require the player to skip a string can cause a gap in the sound. It is better to shift so that the player's bow has less distance to travel. Figure 10.17 is an example of a passage that contains an awkward string crossing if performed in first position (I). The bowing is awkward because the violinist must cross over the A string in order to play the D string. At a fast tempo, this can be quite difficult to execute.

Figure 10.17 An Example of an Awkward String Crossing

Shifting to third position (III) eliminates this awkward string crossing (see Figure 10.18). Third position also maximizes the number of notes played in a single position (Guideline 1).

Figure 10.18 Shift to Avoid Awkward String Crossings

5. **Avoid open strings to achieve a mature sound.** The string player is able to use vibrato and make subtle intonation adjustments on fingered notes. Vibrato and pitch adjustments cannot be executed on open strings. *French Folk Song* is an example that il-lustrates how shifting can help achieve a more mature sound (Figure 10.19). By shifting to position III to perform this passage, the open E string can be avoided (Figure 10.20).

Figure 10.19 French Folk Song in First Position

Figure 10.20 French Folk Song in Third Position

6. **Tempo and style dictate the final fingering choice.** Faster tempi require an efficient fingering that can be executed cleanly and may include open strings, while slower more lyrical passages call for vibrato, requiring the violinist or violist to shift to avoid open strings. Style is another important variable to consider when selecting a fingering. In particular, tone color affects finger choice. Higher positions on lower strings sound darker, while lower positions on higher strings sound brighter. Brahms's Hungarian Dance No. 5 is an excellent example of an excerpt that is performed only on the G string by professional orchestras to produce a darker color (see Figure 10.21).

Figure 10.21 Brahms's Hungarian Dance No. 5 Performed on the G String

Brahms's Hungarian Dance No. 5 is a piece that is often played by intermediate and advanced high school orchestras. The amount of skill or experience that a player has dictates fingering choice. An intermediate player may use first and third position, landmark positions, to perform this same excerpt rather than attempting to perform the entire passage on one string (see Figure 10.22).

Figure 10.22 Intermediate Fingering for Brahms's Hungarian Dance No. 5

Students who have limited skill shifting may use only first position to perform this passage. First position will not allow the player to produce the stylistic sound associated with this piece but certainly exposes the student to great music during the early stages of instruction (see Figure 10.23).

Figure 10.23 Beginning Fingering for Brahms's Hungarian Dance No. 5

There are numerous variables to consider when selecting appropriate fingerings. Additional considerations include a preference to shift on strong beats rather than weak beats, avoiding shifts that occur during slurs, deliberate shifts during slurs or use of portamento (an audible, expressive shift), and taking opportunities to shift during open strings. Choosing good fingerings is a skill that develops over time with experience.

Memorize these six guidelines and remember that these are only guidelines, not hard rules. For any musical excerpt there may be a variety of fingering options that are acceptable. Personal preference, the individual's proficiency on the instrument, and musical context all guide fingering choices. Go to the online tutorial to practice applying the six guidelines.

LEARNING ACTIVITY 10C (ONLINE TUTORIAL 3: PRACTICE CHOOSING VIOLIN AND VIOLA FINGERINGS)

Violin Tutorial 3—http://aim-ed.com/experiments/violindemo/tutorial3
Viola Tutorial 3—http://aim-ed.com/experiments/violademo/tutorial3/

NOTES

1.   Bornoff, G. (1948). *Finger patterns: A basic method for violin.* Toronto, Canada: Gordon V. Thompson.
2.   Bornoff, G. (1949). *Finger patterns: A basic method for viola.* Toronto, Canada: Gordon V. Thompson.

REFERENCES

Allen, M., Gillespie, R. & Tellejohn Hayes, P. (2004). *Essential technique for strings 2000.* Milwaukee, WI: Hal Leonard Corporation.

Anderson, G. & Frost, R. (2008). *All for strings.* Books 1–3. San Diego, CA: Neil A. Kjos Music Company.

Brungard, K. D., Alexander, M., Anderson, G., Dackow, S. & Witt, A. (2004). *Orchestra expressions.* Books 1–2. Van Nuys, CA: Alfred Music.

Dabczynski, A. J., Meyer, R. & Phillips, B. (2002). *String explorer.* Books 1–2. Van Nuys, CA: Highland Etling.

Del Borgo, E. (2008). *Foundations for strings.* Greensboro, NC: C. Alan Publishing.

Dillon, J., Kjelland, J. & O'Reilly, J. (1996). *Strictly strings.* Books 1–3. Van Nuys, CA: Highland Etling.

Erwin, J., Horvath, K., McCashin, R. & Mitchell, B. (2008). *New directions for strings.* Fort Lauderdale, FL: FJH Music Company.

Fischer, S. (1997). *Basics: 300 exercises and practice routines for the violin.* London: Peters Edition Limited.

Fischer, S. (2013). *The violin lesson: A manual for teaching and self-teaching the violin.* London: Peters Edition Limited.

Flesch, C. (1987). *Scale system: Scale exercises in all major and minor keys for daily study.* M. Rostal (Ed.). Berlin 33, Germany: Verlag von Ries & Erler.

Froseth, J. O. & Smith, B. (2003). *Do it! Play strings.* Books 1–2. Chicago, IL: GIA Publications.

Frost, R. & Fischbach, G. (2002). *Artistry in strings*. Books 1–2. San Diego, CA: Neil A. Kjos Music Company.

Galamian, I. (1962). *Principles of violin playing & teaching*. (2nd ed.). Englewood Cliffs, NJ: Prentice-Hall, Inc.

Gazda, D. & Stoutamire, A. (1997). *Spotlight on strings*. San Diego, CA: Neil A. Kjos Music Company.

Hamann, D. & Gillespie, R. (2013). *Strategies for teaching strings*. (3rd ed.). New York, NY: Oxford University Press.

Havas, K. (1964). *The twelve lesson course in a new approach to violin playing, with exercises relating to the fundamental balances*. London: Bosworth.

Kjelland, J. & Dillon, J. (1996). *Strictly strings: Orchestra companion book 3*. Van Nuys, CA: Highland Etling.

Klotman, R. H. (1996). *Teaching strings: Learning to teach through playing*. (2nd ed.). Belmont, CA: Schirmer Books.

Lamb, N. & Cook, S. L. (2002). *Guide to teaching strings*. (7th ed.). New York, NY: McGraw-Hill.

Phillips, B. & Moss, K. (2012). *Sound innovations for string orchestra: Sound development*. Van Nuys: Alfred Music.

Primrose, W. (1976). The viola. In Y. Menhuin & W. Primrose, *Violin and viola*. New York, NY: Schirmer Books.

Schradieck, H. (2011a). *The school of violin technics: Books 1–3 and complete scale studies*. Milwakee, WI: G. Schirmer, Inc.

Schradieck, H. (2011b). *The school of viola technique*. (Vols. 1–2). (L. Pagels, Transcribed.). New York, NY: International Music Company.

Sevcik, O. (1900). *School of technic for violin, Op. 1*. (Vols. 1–4). New York, NY: Carl Fischer.

Sitt, H. (1924). *Practical viola method*. (Revised and Enlarged by W. F. Ambrosio). New York, NY: Carl Fischer, Inc.

Suzuki, S. (2008). *Suzuki violin school*. (Revised ed., Vols. 1–10). Miami, FL: Summy-Birchard, Inc.

Suzuki, S. (2013). *Suzuki viola school*. (Revised ed., Vols. 1–10). Miami, FL: Summy-Birchard, Inc.

Whitcomb, B. (2013). *The advancing violinist's handbook: A guide to practicing and playing the viola*. Bloomington, IN: Authorhouse LLC.

Wohlfahrt, F. (1938). *Foundation studies for the viola*. (Vols. 1–2). (M. J. Isaac & R. C. Lewis, Transcribed.). New York, NY: Carl Fischer.

CHAPTER 11

Cello Fingerings

This chapter aims to provide the prospective string teacher with a basic understanding of the following concepts: (a) left-hand finger patterns, (b) fingerboard geography (the location of the pitches on the fingerboard), and (c) the ability to create basic fingerings for the beginning cellist. The positions on the cello are divided into three large groups: the lower positions (positions ½–IV), the middle or transitional positions (positions V–VII), and the upper positions (VII and higher, also referred to us thumb position). See Figure 11.1.

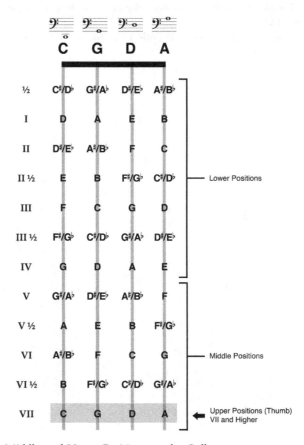

Figure 11.1 Lower, Middle, and Upper Positions on the Cello

This chapter primarily focuses on the finger patterns used in the lower positions because beginning and intermediate cellists use that range of the instrument with the greatest frequency.

CELLO FINGER PATTERNS (POSITIONS ½–IV)

Two basic hand positions are used in the lower positions on the cello: closed and extended. In closed position, the fingers are spaced equidistantly so that one semitone falls between each finger. In closed position, the cellist is able to perform a minor third. Extended position increases the distance between fingers 1 and 2 to accommodate a whole step, thereby allowing the cellist to perform up to a major third before shifting (see Figure 11.2). The technique for transitioning the left hand from closed to extended position is called an extension. There are two types of extensions: forward extensions and backward extensions.

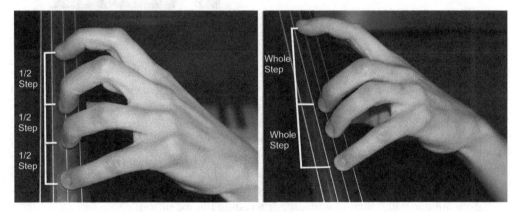

Figure 11.2 Closed and Extended Position on the Cello

Outlined in the following are the three diatonic finger patterns used by cellists in the lower positions:

Finger Pattern 1 (see Figure 11.3) uses fingers 1, 3, and 4 in the closed position to play a whole step followed by a half step.

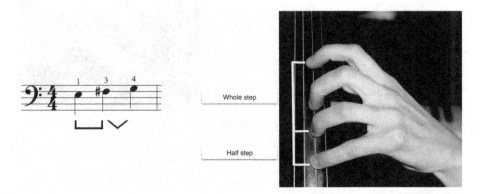

Figure 11.3 Finger Pattern 1—Whole Step, Half Step

Finger Pattern 2 (see Figure 11.4) uses fingers 1, 2, and 4 in the closed position to play a half step followed by a whole step.

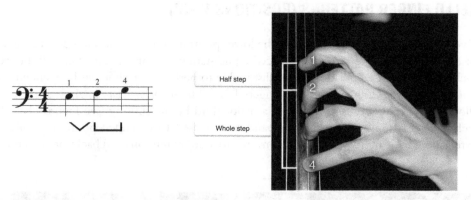

Figure 11.4 Finger Pattern 2—Half Step, Whole Step

Finger Pattern 3 (see Figure 11.5) uses fingers 1, X 2, 4 in the extended position to play two consecutive whole steps. Extensions only occur between fingers one and two because the anatomy of the hand allows for the extension to occur safely between these two fingers. The ligaments and tendons between the other fingers do not have the same level of flexibility. It is inadvisable for students to extend between the other fingers because they risk injuring the hand. For that reason, teachers should take care when teaching extensions to make sure the hand frame is shaped properly. The thumb is positioned behind the second finger in both closed and extended positions. Extensions are generally notated with an X preceding the extension.

These three basic finger patterns can be applied anywhere in the lower positions (½, I, II, II½, III, III½, IV). Before the positions are explained, practice applying the three basic finger patterns in first position.

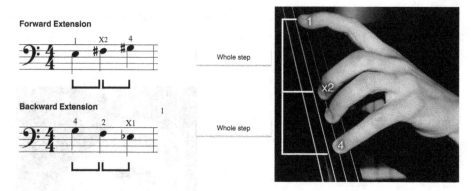

Figure 11.5 Finger Pattern 3—Whole Step, Whole Step

LEARNING ACTIVITY 11A (ONLINE TUTORIAL 1: PRACTICE CELLO FINGER PATTERNS)

Insert Link to Cello Tutorial 1—http://teachingstrings.online/tutorials/cello/Cel loTutorial1/

FINGERBOARD GEOGRAPHY

Fingerboard geography refers to the locations of pitches along the fingerboard. The open strings of the cello are tuned in fifths and include the pitches: C, G, D, and A. The cello fingerboard can be mentally divided into half steps. Each half step along the fingerboard correlates with a position. These positions are ½, I, II, II½, III, III½, IV, V, V½, VI, VI½, and VII (see Figure 11.1).

Seventh position (VII) is an octave higher than the open string. This position also coincides with the halfway harmonic, or the location where the string is divided in half. Natural harmonics on a string instrument occur at the ½, ⅓ and ¼ of each string. By lightly touching (not compressing) the string, the harmonic is produced. The halfway harmonic is significant because thumb position begins in this range of the instrument.

THE POSITIONS

The location of the player's first finger determines the position in which the cellist is considered to be playing. For example, if the cellist's first finger falls on the note E on the D string, then the player is in first (I) or extended first position (Ix) and is able to perform the highlighted notes across the four strings without shifting (see Figure 11.6).

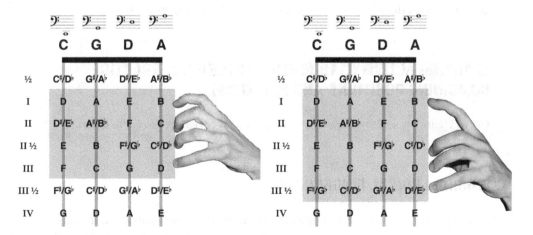

Figure 11.6 First (I) and Second (II) Positions

Whether the cellist is considered to be in first position using a forward extension, or in second position using a backward extension, depends on the context. If the player has been playing in second position and executes a backward extension to play the B, then we would determine that the player was in second position (IIx) with a back extension. If, however, the player was performing in the key of B major and executed a forward extension to perform the C# and D#, then the player would be in first position (Ix) using a forward extension.

Here is another example. If the cellist's first finger falls on the note F on the D string, then the player is in second position (II) or extended second position (IIx) and is able to perform the following notes across the four strings (see Figure 11.7).

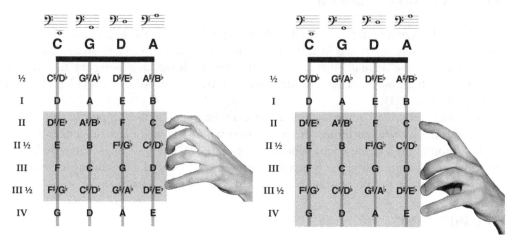

Figure 11.7 Position II and Position IIx

To further illustrate this concept, imagine that the cellist has fourth finger on the pitch "G" on the A string. On what note would the first finger fall? In closed position, the first finger would fall a minor third below the G, or on the E. Because the location of the first finger is on the E, the player is in fourth position (IV; see Figure 11.8).

LEARNING ACTIVITY 11B (ONLINE TUTORIAL 2: PRACTICE COMBINING POSITIONS AND PATTERNS)

Go to Cello Tutorial 2—teachingstrings.online/tutorials/cello/CelloTutorial2/

CHOOSING LOGICAL FINGERINGS

The same pitch can be performed by a cellist in more than one location on the fingerboard, and with more than one finger (1, 2, 3, or 4). For example, the open A string is the same pitch as the A in position IV on the D string (see Figure 11.9).

Because the pitches can be played in more than one location, and with fingers 1, 2, 3, or 4, string players have options to consider as they determine which fingering to use. Here

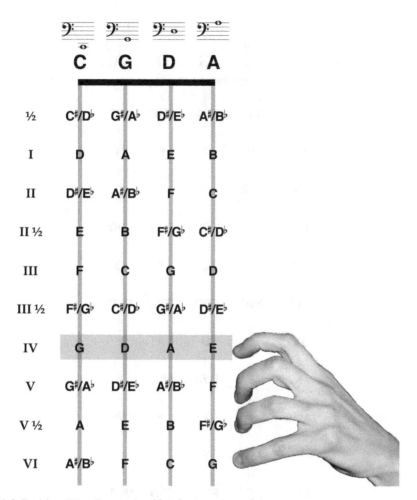

Figure 11.8 Position IV as Determined by the Location of the First Finger

are six basic guidelines that can help you determine which finger, position, and string to use.

SIX GUIDELINES FOR CELLO FINGERINGS

1. **Maximize the number of notes you can play in a single position**. Economy of motion is important on all stringed instruments. Choosing a fingering that limits the number of shifts and maximizes the number of notes played in a single position is ideal. For example, fourth position is the most logical choice for the following excerpt because it allows the player to remain in one position (see Figure 11.10).

If the same melodic pattern began on a different note, the cellist would choose another position for this passage to avoid shifting (see Figure 11.11).

2. **Near shifts are better than far shifts.** When shifting is necessary, choose the position that minimizes the physical distance between pitches. A rule of thumb is to shift

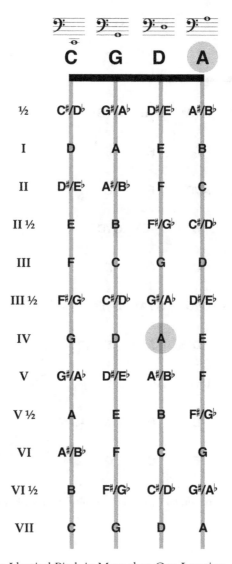

Figure 11.9 Example of the Identical Pitch in More than One Location.

Figure 11.10 Position IV with Finger Pattern 1

Figure 11.11 Position III with Finger Pattern 1

on the smallest interval in the passage while still considering how to maximize the number of notes played in one position (see Figure 11.12).

Figure 11.12 Shifting on the Smallest Musical Interval

3. **Use landmark positions (positions I, III, IV, and VII).** These four positions correspond to the open strings and allow the player to double-check their pitch accuracy. The notes played by the first finger in these positions (or thumb in seventh position) are often referred to as ring tones. When the pitches C, G, D, and A are played in tune, the open string vibrates sympathetically, producing overtones that ring. In Figure 11.13, fourth position is illustrated.

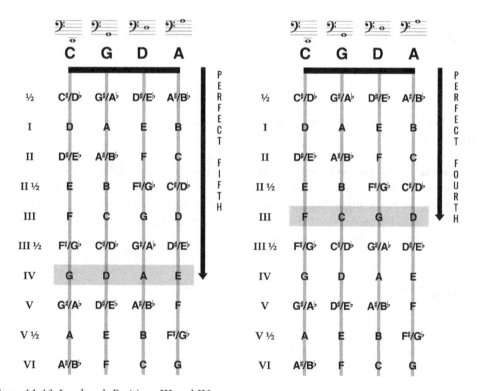

Figure 11.13 Landmark Positions III and IV

Because the strings on the cello are tuned in fifths, the first note in fourth position on any given string is the same pitch as the higher adjacent open string. For example, in fourth position on the D string, the first finger plays the pitch A. A is a perfect fifth above D and is the same pitch as the open A string. These corresponding open strings are what make fourth position a landmark position. In fourth position, players have the ability to check whether their left hand is in tune with the open strings.

Third position is also a landmark position because the first note in third position performs the identical pitch as the lower adjacent open string. For example, the first finger in the third position on the D string is G, the same note as the open G string, only one octave higher. Third position is a perfect fourth higher than the open string (see Figure 11.13).

The beginning of "Twinkle" is a good example that illustrates when using landmark positions may be preferred over near shifts, particularly for beginners (see Figure 11.14).

Figure 11.14 Twinkle Using Landmark Position IV

Notice that the passage begins in first position and then indicates that the player should shift to fourth position. III½ position is nearer, so the cellist could play the passage as shown in Figure 11.15.

Figure 11.15 Twinkle Using Position III½

The beginning cellist will have more success shifting to position IV because it is a landmark position.

4. **Shift to avoid awkward string crossings.** Passages that require the player to skip a string can cause a gap in the sound. It is better to shift so that the player's bow has less distance to travel. Figure 11.16 is an example of an awkward string crossing that requires the cellist to skip over the D string in order to play the G string. At a fast tempo, this can be quite difficult to execute.

Figure 11.16 Example of an Awkward String Crossing

This passage can be made easier if the cellist performs the B on the D string in position IV (see Figure 11.17).

Figure 11.17 Example of Shifting to Avoid an Awkward String Crossing

5. **Avoid open strings to achieve a mature sound.** The string player is able to use vibrato and make subtle intonation adjustments on fingered notes. Vibrato and pitch adjustments cannot be executed on an open string. "Frere Jacques" is an example that illustrates how shifting can help achieve a more mature sound. By shifting to position II ½ in measures three and four, the open A string can be avoided (see Figures 11.18 and 11.19).

Figure 11.18 Frere Jacques in Position I

Figure 11.19 Frere Jacques in Positions I and II½

6. **Tempo and style dictate the final fingering choice.** Faster tempi require an efficient fingering that can be executed cleanly (see Figure 11.20), while slower more lyrical passages call for vibrato, requiring the cellist to shift to avoid open strings (see Figure 11.21). Other stylistic variables include tone color (higher positions on lower strings sound darker and lower positions on higher strings sound brighter) and the use of portamento—when an audible slide shifting from one note to the next is desired. Finally, cellists prefer to shift on strong rather than weak beats. Shifting on strong beats improves the coordination between the left and right hand. As a general rule, string players attempt to avoid shifts during slurs, but this is not always possible.

Figure 11.20 Faster Passage Using Open Strings

Figure 11.21 Lyrical Passage Shifting to Avoid the Open A String

> Note: Using the same finger for three or more notes in a row is considered an illegal maneuver on any string instrument.

Memorize these six guidelines. Remember that these are only guidelines and not hard rules. For any musical excerpt there may be a variety of fingering options that are acceptable.

Personal preference, the individual's proficiency on the instrument, and musical context all guide fingering choices. Go to the online tutorial to practice applying the six guidelines.

LEARNING ACTIVITY 11C (ONLINE TUTORIAL 3: CHOOSING CELLO FINGERINGS)

[Insert Cello Tutorial 3: http://teachingstrings.online/tutorials/cello/CelloTutorial3/]

REFERENCES

Alexanian, D., Casals, P. & Geber D. (2003). *Complete cello technique: The classic treatise on cello theory and practice*. Mineola, NY: Dover Publications.

Allen, M., Gillespie, R. & Hayes, P. T. (2004). *Essential technique 2000 for strings*. Milwaukee, WI: Hal Leonard Corporation.

Feuillard, L. R. (1929). *Methode du jeune violincelliste*. (S. Patte, Trans.). Nice, France: Edition Delrieu.

Horsfall, J. (1974). *Teaching the cello to groups*. Ely House, London: Oxford University Press.

Mantel, G. (1975). *Cello technique*. (B. H. Thiem, Trans.). Don Mills, ON: Indiana University Press. (Original work published in 1972).

Matz, R. (1974). *The complete cellist: Book 1*. M. S. Silverberg (Ed.). (L. Aronson, Trans.). New York, NY: Tetra Music Corporation.

Pleeth, W. (1982). *Cello*. N. Pyron (Ed.). New York, NY: Schirmer Books.

Potter, L. (1973). *The art of cello playing*. (Revised ed.). Evanston, IL: Summy-Birchard Company.

Starker, J. (1965). *An organized method of string playing: Violoncello exercises for the left hand*. New York, NY: Peer International Corporation.

CHAPTER 12

Bass Fingerings

Bass pedagogy is the most diverse of the four bowed stringed instruments and includes many different viewpoints. For that reason, teachers must make a number of decisions in terms of which overarching philosophy they will use to teach the instrument. For example, the teacher must decide whether the students will learn to play the bass standing or seated or to use a French or German bow (see Chapters 4 and 6). One of the best ways for a novice teacher to decide which method to use is by deferring to the most experienced string teacher in the community. If there is a bass teacher who provides private lessons in the area, then it makes sense to develop a relationship with that person and create a consistent pedagogical approach that incorporates his or her viewpoints. This chapter focuses on bass finger patterns and positions. The prospective string teacher should develop a basic understanding of the following concepts: (a) left-hand finger patterns (b) fingerboard geography (the location of the pitches on the fingerboard), (c) positions, (d) combining the patterns and positions, and (e) the ability to choose basic fingerings for the beginning bassist.

More than one fingering system exists for the string bass, but most heterogeneous method books use the fingering system outlined by Franz Simandl (1968) in the *New Method for the Double Bass*.[1] The Simandl method organizes the bass finger patterns into two large groups: the three basic finger patterns that are utilized in the lower positions and the finger patterns used in the upper positions (thumb position). This chapter focuses on the finger patterns and positions used in the lower range; the range most frequently used by bassists in elementary, middle, and high school.

BASS FINGER PATTERNS

Because the bass is a large instrument, the physical distance between pitches is also large. In the lower positions, bass players use fingers 1, 2, and 4. The third finger is not used independently in the lower positions but, rather, functions as additional support for the fourth finger.

This hand frame is commonly referred to as "K-position" because the extended space between fingers 1 and 2 approximates the shape of a K (see Figure 12.1). Using this hand frame, the bass player is able to perform three fingering options:

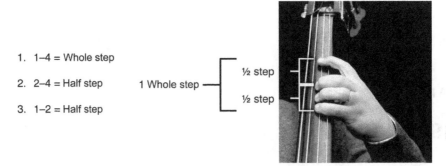

1. 1–4 = Whole step

2. 2–4 = Half step

3. 1–2 = Half step

1 Whole step
½ step
½ step

Figure 12.1 K-position

1. **Finger Pattern 1** (see Figure 12.2) is called the 1–4 pattern and permits the bass player to perform one whole step.

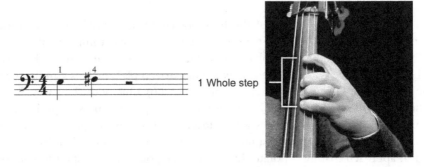

1 Whole step

Figure 12.2 1–4 Finger Pattern in Position I on the D String

2. **Finger Pattern 2** (see Figure 12.3) is called the 2–4 finger pattern and allows the bassist to play a half step.

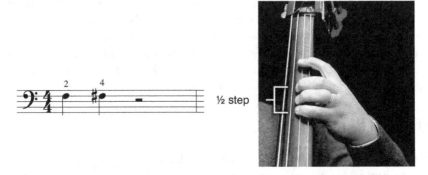

½ step

Figure 12.3 2–4 Finger Pattern in Position I on the D String

3. **Finger Pattern 3** (see Figure 12.4) is called the 1–2 finger pattern and allows the bassist to play a half step.

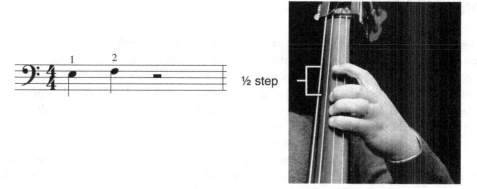

Figure 12.4 1–2 Finger Pattern in Position I on the D String

This basic hand position is mobile and shifts to play in any location and on any string in the lower positions. Because of the physical distances between pitches on the bass fingerboard, in general it is only possible to play the musical distance of one whole step in the lower positions prior to shifting or crossing strings. By adding an open string, the bassist can increase this range to a major third (see Figure 12.5).

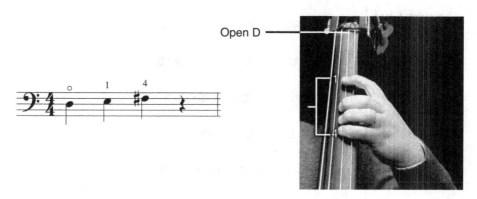

Figure 12.5 The Open String Combined with the 1–4 Finger Pattern

LEARNING ACTIVITY 12A (ONLINE TUTORIAL 1: PRACTICE BASS FINGER PATTERNS)

Practice selecting bass finger patterns. Send a screenshot of the final frame to your teacher.

http://teachingstrings.online/tutorials/bass/BassTutorial1/

FINGERBOARD GEOGRAPHY

The open strings of the double bass are tuned in fourths and include the pitches: E, A, D, and G. The string bass is a transposing instrument; the performed notes sound an octave lower than written. On a string instrument, as the fingers compress the string, the vibrating portion of the string is shortened causing the string to vibrate more rapidly, thus producing a higher pitch. The bass fingerboard can be mentally organized by ascending half steps. To help illustrate the location of the pitches, imaginary frets may be placed on the bass fingerboard, much like finger placement markers for beginners. The location of the pitches along the fingerboard is referred to by string players as fingerboard geography. These imaginary frets divide the fingerboard into positions by half steps. The positions on the string bass include ½, I, II, II½, III, III½, IV, V, V½, VI, VI½, and VII (see Figure 12.6). The bass player's hand shifts to reach higher notes in higher positions.

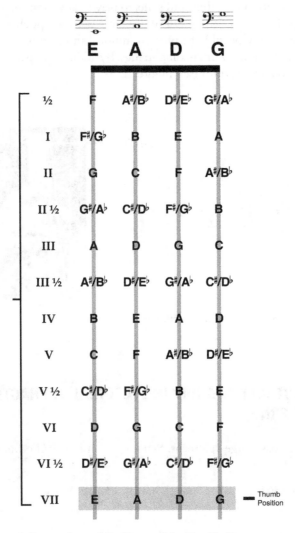

Figure 12.6 Fingerboard Geography and Positions of the Double Bass

Seventh position is one octave higher than the open string. For example, the octave G in seventh position on the G string is the halfway harmonic on the bass, meaning the location where the string is divided in half. Natural harmonics on a string instrument occur at the ½, ⅓ and ¼ of each string. By lightly touching (not compressing) the string, the harmonic is produced. The halfway harmonic is the location when the bassist begins to use thumb position and third finger. This is where the lower positions on the bass end, and the upper positions begin.

The location of the player's first finger determines the position in which the bassist is playing. For instance, when the bassist's first finger falls on the note F on the E string, then the player is in ½ position and is able to perform the highlighted notes across the four strings without shifting. Similarly, if the bassist's first finger is performing the note A on the G string, the player is in first position and is able to perform the highlighted notes across the four strings without shifting (see Figure 12.7).

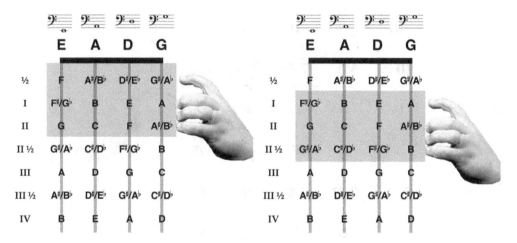

Figure 12.7 Positions ½ and I on the Double Bass

Imagine that the bassist has his or her fourth finger on the pitch D on the G string (see Figure 12.8). On what note would the first finger fall? Because the bassist uses fingers 1, 2, and 4, and we know that the musical distance between 1 and 4 is a whole step, we can deduce that the bassists' first finger is on the pitch C. The bassist is in third position.

LEARNING ACTIVITY 12B (ONLINE TUTORIAL 2: PRACTICE BASS PATTERNS AND POSITIONS)

Practice selecting bass finger patterns. Send a screenshot of the final frame to your teacher.

http://teachingstrings.online/tutorials/bass/BassTutorial2/

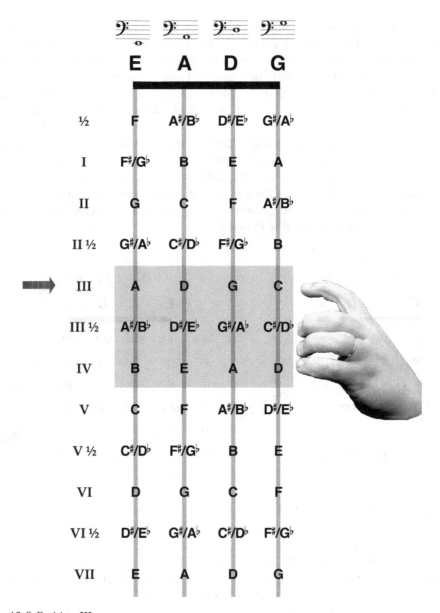

Figure 12.8 Position III

COMBINING PATTERNS AND POSITIONS FOR BASS PLAYERS

Bass students must combine the basic finger patterns and positions almost immediately in order to play beginning scales and simple songs. The following are the combined patterns and positions regularly presented in beginning string method books. The pattern combinations presented here can be played on any string; however, most heterogeneous string method books present the bass finger patterns in the following sequence: D major, G major, and C major. This typical progression is designed to include all four instruments simultaneously (violin, viola, cello, and bass). Method books written to teach in homogeneous settings may sequence materials differently than methods written for heterogeneous group settings. For example, the Suzuki method begins violin players in the key of A major and cello, viola, and bass in the key of D major. The combinations of patterns, open strings, and shifting presented in this chapter explain the sequence of instruction in a class geared toward group instruction where violins, violas, and cellos are also present.

The D Major Scale

The first notes typically introduced in heterogeneous string method books are D, E, F#, and G. By combining the open D and G string with the 1–4 finger pattern, the bassist is able to play the first tetrachord of the D major scale (see Figure 12.9).

After the students are able to play the 1–4 finger pattern on the D string (including three-note songs), this finger pattern is transferred to the G string. To play the second tetrachord of the D major scale (A, B, C#, D), bass players need to shift their hand from first to third position. The shift illustrated in Figure 12.10 is taught almost immediately in the beginning strings class so that the bassists are able to play the D major scale along with the

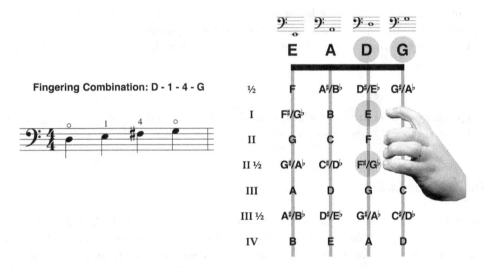

Figure 12.9 Fingering Combination D 1–4 G

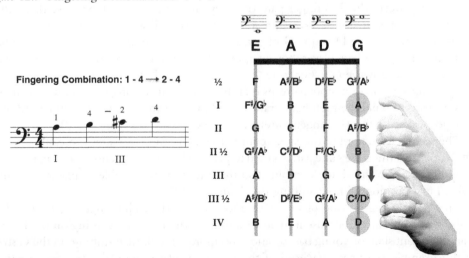

Figure 12.10 Fingering Combination 1–4, Half-step Shift, 2–4

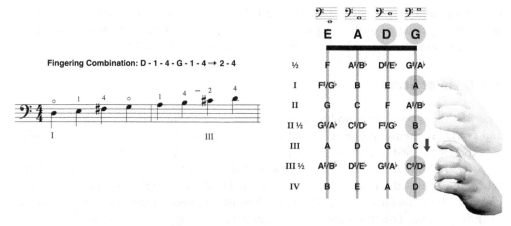

Figure 12.11 Fingering for the D Major Scale

violins, violas, and cellos. In order to play A, B, C#, D, the bassist must use the 1–4 finger pattern, shift to third position, then play the 2–4 finger pattern.

Using the two fingering combinations outlined earlier, the bassist is able to play the D scale (see Figure 12.11).

Go here to explore the fingerings of the D major scale online:
http://teachingstrings.online/tutorials/bass/scalesandchart/

The G Major Scale

Once students are able to perform the D scale and simple songs in the key of D major, the G major scale is generally introduced. Teaching the D scale, then immediately the G scale, is a logical sequence for violin, viola, and cello students because the fingerings for the D and G major scales are identical. For example, once violinists or violists learn to play their first finger pattern (the 2–3 finger pattern), they are immediately able to use that pattern to play D major, G major, and A major scales. Similarly, cellists' first finger pattern (1, 3, 4) can be used to play the D major, G major, and C major scales by simply moving the hand over one string. The bass player, however, must learn a new fingering and a new pattern combination to play the G major scale.

Teaching scales in four-note patterns is fairly common in a string class because it encourages students to build their left hand frame and think in patterns. The first tetrachord of the G major scale uses the 1–2 finger pattern in first position (see Figure 12.12).

The second tetrachord of this scale requires the use of the 1–4 pattern to easily reach the F#. Notice that this is the same pattern used to play the D major tetrachord (see Figure 12.13).

These two tetrachords are combined so that the students are able to play the G major scale in first position without shifting (see Figure 12.14).

The G scale can also be played with another fingering. This fingering is considered slightly more advanced because it includes a shift on the D string. Shifting on the D string is an important skill for young bassists and is no more difficult than shifting on the G string. In this example, the first tetrachord of the G scale is played with the 1–2 finger pattern,

Fingering Combination: 2 - A - 1 - 2

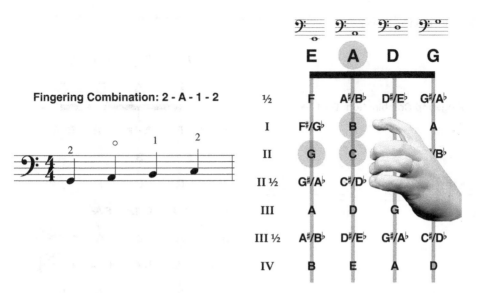

Figure 12.12 Fingering Combination for the G Major Tetrachord

Fingering Combination: D - 1 - 4 - G

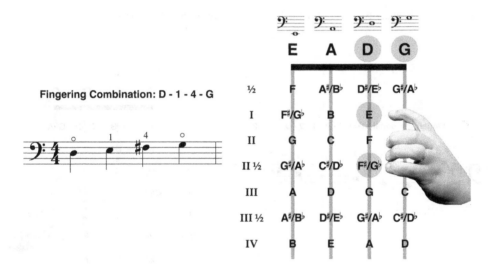

Figure 12.13 Fingering for Second Half of the G Major Scale

Fingering Combination: 2 - A - 1 - 2 - D - 1 - 4 - G

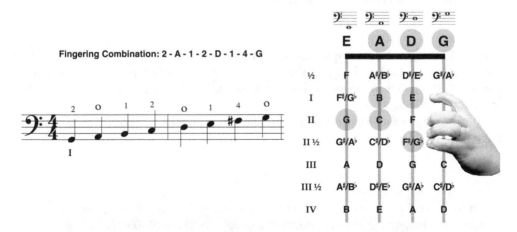

Figure 12.14 Fingering for the G Major Scale

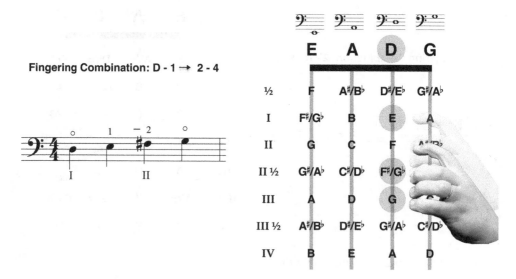

Figure 12.15 Alternate Fingering for the Second Octave of the G Major Scale

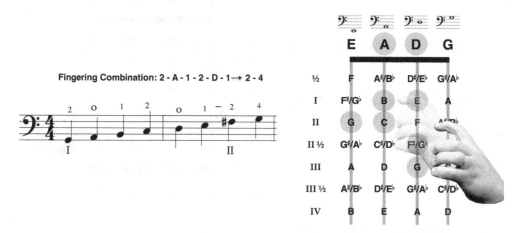

Figure 12.16 Alternate Fingering for the G Major Scale

as it was in the previous example. The second tetrachord of the G major scale has another fingering option. Rather than play the notes D, E, F#, G in first position, the player can play D (0), E (1), shift to second position, and use the 2–4 finger pattern to play the F# (2) and D (4; see Figure 12.15).

Together, these fingering combinations allow the player to perform the G scale (see Figure 12.16).

Go to the online tutorial to see the two fingering options for the G major scale: http://teachingstrings.online/tutorials/bass/scalesandchart–NoID/

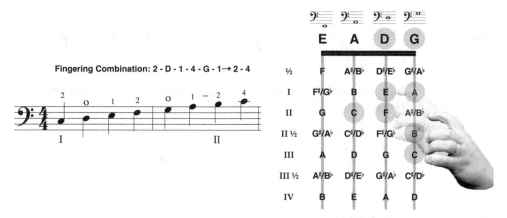

Fingering Combination: 2 - D - 1 - 4 - G - 1→ 2 - 4

Figure 12.17 Fingering for the C Major Scale

The C Major Scale

The C major scale uses the same fingering as the second G major scale fingering presented earlier. At this point in instruction, the violinist and violists must learn a new finger pattern (the 1–2 pattern). Cellists and bassists can simply transfer the fingering that they used for the G major scale over one string. Bass players begin the C major scale by using second finger on the A string (see Figure 12.17).

Go to the online tutorial to view an animation of this fingering for the C major scale. http://teachingstrings.online/tutorials/bass/scalesandchart/

CHOOSING LOGICAL FINGERINGS

Scales provide a basic framework for fingerings, but ultimately the musical context dictates which fingering is best. String players usually have more than one fingering option for any sequence of notes as you may have observed in the G major scale. The same pitch can be performed on a string instrument in more than one location. Furthermore, each pitch may be played with either finger 1, 2, or 4. Because the pitches can be played in more than one location and with fingers 1, 2, or 4, the string player has options to consider as they determine which fingering to use. So, how do you choose the best fingering? Here are six basic guidelines that can help you make decisions about which finger, position, and string to use.

Six Guidelines for Bass Fingerings

1. **Maximize the number of notes you can play in a single position.** To play as many notes in a single position as possible, most bass players prefer to ascend using first finger shifts because fingers 2 and 4 remain available to play the next pitches. For the same reason, bass players generally prefer to descend using fourth finger shifts because fingers 1 and 2 are available to play the next pitches (see Figure 12.18). Plan ahead to limit the number of shifts and maximize notes in each position.

The fingering in the first example in Figure 12.19 does not follow this guideline. Although a bass player technically *can* play this fingering, it requires the bassist to shift twice, making

Figure 12.18 An Example of Maximizing Notes in a Single Position by Shifting up to First Finger and Back to Fourth Finger

Figure 12.19 Maximize Notes and Minimize Shift

the passage unnecessarily awkward. This fingering in the second example is better because it maximizes the number of notes in each position and requires fewer shifts.

2. **Near shifts are better than far shifts.** When shifting is necessary, choose the position that minimizes the physical distance between pitches while still maximizing the number of notes played in one position (Guidelines 1 and 2). Efficiency is better than leaping around the fingerboard. *French Folk Song* is a good example that illustrates the use of near positions (see Figure 12.20).

Figure 12.20 An Example of Using Near Positions

It makes more sense for the bassist to shift from position III to position II½ than it does for the bass player to shift back to first position to play only one note. By shifting to position II½, the left hand travels less distance and is more efficient.

3. **Use landmark positions (positions I, III, IV, and VII).** Landmark positions on a string instrument are more secure positions that tend to be used with greater frequency because these positions correspond to an open string. For example, first position is nearest to the open string, which subsequently provides a stable pitch for the player to build on—assuming that the open strings are in tune.

Third, fourth, and seventh positions also correspond to the open strings, giving the player a way to check pitch accuracy. The notes played by the first finger in these positions (or thumb in seventh position) are often referred to as "ring tones." Ring tones are pitches that double an open string. When the pitches E, A, D, and G are played in tune, the open string vibrates sympathetically, producing overtones that "ring."

Because the strings on the bass are tuned in fourths, the first note in third position on any given string is the same pitch as the higher adjacent open string. For example, in third position on the D string, the first finger plays the pitch G. G is a perfect fourth above D and is the same pitch as the open G string. These corresponding open strings are what make third position a landmark position. In third position, the player has the ability to check whether their left hand is in tune with the open strings.

Fourth position is also a landmark position because the first note in fourth position performs the identical pitch as the lower adjacent open string. For example, the first finger in fourth position on the G string is D, the same note as the open D string, only one octave higher. Fourth position is a perfect fifth higher than the open strings (see Figure 12.21).

The beginning of "Frere Jacques" is an example that illustrates when using landmark positions may be preferred over near shifts for beginners (see Figure 12.22).

Notice that the passage begins in first position then indicates that the player should shift to third position. In the fourth measure, II½ position is nearer, but the C# has already been played in the previous measure with a fourth finger in first position. Consequently, it makes sense to keep the pattern consistent and use first and third positions to play this passage. Different players sometimes prefer different fingerings. Some bass players may actually prefer the fingering option in parenthesis that uses a near shift. Both fingerings are acceptable options. When choosing fingerings, try to find the option that works best for your students.

4. **Shift to avoid awkward string crossings.** Passages that require the player to skip a string can cause a gap in the sound. It is better to shift so that the player's bow has less distance to travel. Below is an example of an awkward string crossing that requires the bassist to skip over the D string in order to play the A if they attempt to play the passage in first position with the first finger on the G string. At a fast tempo, this can be quite difficult to execute (Figure 12.23). This string crossing can be made easier if the bassist plays the A on the D string using position III, III½ or IV. By performing the A on the D string, the distance that the bow needs to travel to perform the string crossing is reduced, making the passage easier to play.

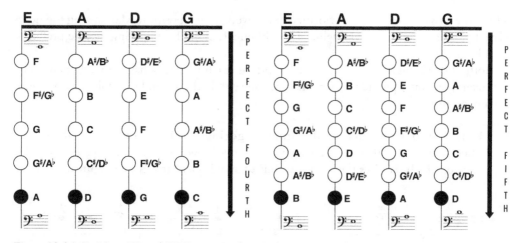

Figure 12.21 Positions III and IV Correspond to Open Strings and Can Provide a Landmark for the Left Hand

Figure 12.22 Using Landmark Positions

Whether the bassist chooses to play the A in position III, III½, or IV depends on the next pitch or pitches. If the next pitch is a G, then the bass player would choose to play this measure in third position so that it is possible to maximize the number of notes played in one position and minimize shifts (Example A), whereas, if the next pitch is a B or B♭, the bassist would choose position IV.

Figure 12.23 Avoiding Awkward String Crossings

Figure 12.24 Avoiding String Crossings and Maximizing Notes in a Single Position

5. **Avoid open strings to achieve a mature tone.** The string player is able to use vibrato and make subtle intonation adjustments on fingered notes. Vibrato and pitch adjustments cannot be executed on an open string. Figure 12.25 illustrates Guideline 4: Avoiding string crossings and Guideline 5: Avoiding open strings. A more advanced player would likely choose to perform this passage all on the D string.

This same passage can also be performed exclusively in first position: Maximizing the notes played in a single position (Guideline 1; see Figure 12.26). This fingering may be preferred for a beginner.

Both of these fingerings are acceptable options. Each fingering has its own benefits. The first example would provide a more mature tone, while the second example may be easier for a beginner.

6. **Tempo and style dictate the final fingering choice.** Faster tempi require an efficient fingering that can be executed cleanly. Slower more lyrical passages call for vibrato, which requires the bassist to shift to avoid open strings (see Figure 12.27).

Figure 12.25 Shifting to Avoid Open Strings

Figure 12.26 *Baccarole* in First Position

Figure 12.27 Faster Passages May Use Open Strings. Slower Passages Should Be Performed with Vibrato and the Player May Shift to Avoid Open Strings

String players also choose different fingerings to produce various tone colors. Open strings and passages executed in lower positions tend to be associated with a brighter sound, while notes played on lower strings in higher positions are associated with a darker sound. On the string bass, players tend to avoid playing in higher positions on the lower strings because it is difficult to produce a clear tone unless the instrument itself is set up extremely well.

> Note: Using the same finger for three or more notes in a row is considered an illegal maneuver on any string instrument.

LEARNING ACTIVITY 12C (ONLINE TUTORIAL 3: CHOOSING BASS FINGERINGS)

Memorize the six guidelines. Remember that these are only guidelines and not hard rules. Numerous contextual variables and individual preference impacts fingering choices.

Insert link to Bass tutorial 3—http://teachingstrings.online/tutorials/bass/BassTutorial3/

NOTE

1. Simandl, F. (1968). *New method for string bass*. S. Sankey (Ed.). New York, NY: International Music Company.

REFERENCES

Allen, M., Gillespie, R. & Tellejohn Hayes, P. (2004). *Essential technique for strings 2000*. Milwaukee, WI: Hal Leonard Corporation.

Anderson, G. & Frost, R. (2008). *All for strings*. Books 1–3. San Diego, CA: Neil A. Kjos Music Company.

Bornoff, G. (1951). *Finger patterns for string bass: A basic method for string bass*. Toronto, Canada: Gordon V. Thompson Inc.

Brungard, K. D., Alexander, M., Anderson, G., Dackow, S. & Witt, A. (2004). *Orchestra expressions*. Books 1–2. Van Nuys, CA: Alfred Music.

Dabczynski, A. J., Meyer, R. & Phillips, B. (2002). *String explorer*. Books 1–2. Van Nuys, CA: Highland Etling.

Del Borgo, E. (2008). *Foundations for Strings*. Greensboro, NC: C. Alan Publishing.

Dillon, J., Kjelland, J. & O'Reilly, J. (1996). *Strictly strings*. Books 1–3. Van Nuys, CA: Highland Etling.

Erwin, J., Horvath, K., McCashin, R. & Mitchell, B. (2008). *New directions for strings*. Fort Lauderdale, FL: FJH Music Company.

Froseth, J. O. & Smith, B. (2003). *Do it! Play strings*. Books 1–2. Chicago, IL: GIA Publications.

Frost, R. & Fischbach, G. (2002). *Artistry in strings*. Books 1–2. San Diego, CA: Neil A. Kjos Music Company.

Green, E. A. H. (1999). *Teaching stringed instruments in classes*. Fairfax, VA: American String Teachers Association.

Hamann, D. L. & Gillespie, R. (2013). *Strategies for teaching strings: Building a successful string and orchestra program*. (3rd ed.). Oxford, New York: Oxford University Press.

Kjelland, J. & Dillon, J. (1996). *Strictly strings: Orchestra companion*. Book 3. Van Nuys, CA: Highland Etling.

Klotman, R. H. (1996). *Teaching strings: Learning to teach through playing*. (2nd ed.). Belmont, CA: Schirmer Books.

Lamb, N. & Cook, S. L. (2002). *Guide to teaching strings*. (7th ed.). New York, NY: McGraw-Hill.

Phillips, B. & Moss, K. (2012). *Sound innovations for string orchestra: Sound development*. Van Nuys: Alfred Music.

Rolland, P., Mutchler, M. & Hellebrandt, F. (2010). *The teaching of action in string playing*. (3rd ed.). Urbana, IL: Illinois String Research.

Suzuki, S. (2002). *Suzuki bass school*. (Revised ed., Vols. 1–5). Van Nuys, CA: Summy-Birchard, Inc.

Vance, G. (2000). *Progressive repertoire for the double bass*. (Vols. 1–5). New York, NY: Carl Fischer, LLC.

CHAPTER 13

Shifting and Vibrato

The main purpose of this text is to lay the foundations for string instruction. Shifting and vibrato are intermediate skills for which there are numerous resources, and I strongly encourage additional exploration of these topics. Shifting and vibrato are usually taught once students have established a good left-hand position with consistent intonation. However, there are pre-shifting and pre-vibrato exercises that should be included during initial instruction. The exercises included in this chapter are introductory activities. Shifting and vibrato both require that students are able to hold their instrument for brief periods without the use of the left hand. Endeavor to teach a left-hand frame that is balanced, flexible, and free of tension so that students are prepared to shift and vibrate.

TEACH SHIFTING FROM THE FIRST YEAR

One of the very best ways to reinforce good instrument position and correct left-hand shape is by incorporating shifting activities early because students will not be able to shift if they are holding the instrument incorrectly. Rolland advocated shaping the students' left hand with the pinky over the halfway harmonic.[1] The *Teaching Action in String Playing* DVD shows students exploring various areas of the fingerboard through pinky plucks, pinky strums, and harmonics. Many method books begin bassists in third rather than first position, so bassists frequently shift during the first year of instruction. Some pedagogues even begin violinists and violists in third position.[2] Books designed for heterogeneous instruction begin with the open strings and in the key of D specifically to accommodate all the instruments simultaneously. Be aware that there are many systems from which to choose.

Exercises that include motions to release tension and increase flexibility benefit the students in addition to preparing them for shifting. Pre-shifting exercises include activities such as pinky strums, pinky plucks, and D Scale in Canon (see Chapter 5). The following pre-shifting exercises will further prepare students for shifting and can be included during the first and second year of instruction.

Pre-Shifting Exercises

3.1 1. Shuttles: Have students practice plucking with their pinky in first position; then continue plucking as they slide their left hand toward the bridge and back toward the scroll.

13.2 ▶ 2. Riding the rails: Place the first finger on the lowest string, second finger on the next string, on so on so that all four fingers are resting on a string. Have the students slide their hand slowly towards the bridge and then back toward the scroll. The thumb travels with the hand, and the wrist is straight. Have students practice this exercise slowly so that their shift is smooth and each of their four fingers stay in contact with the string.

13.3 ▶ 3. Ski jumps (cello and bass): Asking cello and bass students to regularly touch their bridge, then slide back to first position will encourage the proper elbow height. The arm should not run into the body of the instrument as students attempt to shift to the bridge. In the following video, students are performing ski jumps where they slide up the string to touch the bridge.

13.4 ▶ 4. Harmonics: Perform the open string, then slide the left hand to play the halfway harmonic (violins and violas should use fourth finger; cellos and basses should perform the halfway harmonic with third finger). Performing harmonics reinforces a loose thumb and relaxed hand because the string is not compressed, and the note cannot speak if the student squeezes.

13.5 ▶ 5. Ghosting: Have students tremolo with their bow and play harmonics up and down the string. Sliding the left hand smoothly while executing the tremolo with the right hand will increase right and left-hand independence. Further, the students shifting finger should remain slightly in contact with the string during shifts. By performing harmonic sirens, students will practice the correct shifting motion.

13.6 ▶ 6. Sirens: Students can practice sliding with the string compressed, maintaining a straight wrist and loose thumb. Sliding while compressing the string provides the opportunity for students to hear the musical distance of shifts. Eventually, combining a ghosting motion with the siren will promote light, smooth, accurate shifts.

13.7 ▶ 7. Practice intervals: Have students perform with their first fingers in first position, then slide to third position. This interval is a minor third for all of the instruments. Next, slide from first position to fourth position, a perfect fourth; then first to fifth position, a perfect fifth; and so on.

13.8 ▶ 8. Perform one finger scales: Practice one octave scales using only the first finger to play every note. This promotes ear training as well as proper shifting.

Common Shifting Elements

1. The thumb should remain loose and move with the hand as the hand shifts.
2. During the shift, the students should maintain light contact with the string and avoid jumping to the new note. The distance of the shift needs to be felt physically. If the shift is too audible, this is because the student is squeezing and needs to release the left hand.
3. The left-hand wrist should remain straight during the shift. Maintaining a consistent hand frame is important for accurate intonation.

TEACH VIBRATO FROM THE FIRST YEAR OF INSTRUCTION

Vibrato frequently separates beginners from intermediate and more advanced players. Vibrato is produced by manipulating the pitch on a string instrument and oscillates both above and below the intended pitch.[3] Teaching vibrato in a heterogeneous classroom is challenging as violinists and violists vibrate somewhat differently than cellists and bassists, so different exercises are needed for the different instruments. As with shifting, proper instrument position must be established in order for students to successfully vibrate. The left hand needs to be balanced and free of tension. If students are unable to hold the instrument for brief periods without the left hand, vibrato will be difficult, if not impossible to perform. The following exercises should be introduced early to the students.

Pre-Vibrato Exercises

Violin and Viola

1. Flexible knuckles: The student should be able to flex the first knuckle joint of each finger easily. Make a circle with the index finger and thumb. Practice flexing the first knuckle joint. Repeat this exercise on each finger.

2. Transfer the flexible knuckles to the instrument (violin and viola): Violinists and violists should place their finger on the body of the instrument with the fingernail facing towards the bridge. Place the finger in a boxed position with the side of the finger touching the fingerboard. The fingerboard can act as a guide for this flexibility exercise. Using a primarily backward motion, students should straighten then return to a boxed finger position.

3. Manual assist: Sometimes students may need some assistance in executing the correct motion. Violin and viola players can assist themselves by holding their left wrist with their right hand. (See Video 13.12)

4. Pull away (violin and viola): The base knuckle joint of the index finger must release so that the hand has the mobility to vibrate (this motion is subtle and should be a barely visible movement).[4] This motion occurs in the thumb joint of the left hand, one of the many reasons that the thumb cannot squeeze and must remain loose.

5. Forward taps: Place the thumb at the base of the neck where it connects with the instrument. Tap rhythm patterns on the middle strings of the violin or viola using a swinging motion from the wrist. This exercise can be introduced in the first few weeks of class. Tapping the rhythms to various songs can be beneficial for musicianship skills as well as the development of vibrato.

Cello and Bass

1. Flexible knuckles: The student should be able to flex the first knuckle joint of each finger easily. Make a circle with the index finger and thumb. Practice flexing the first knuckle joint. Repeat this exercise on each finger. This activity is primarily for violin and viola players; however, cello and bass students will also benefit because flexibility in this joint is required when vibrating in thumb position.

2. Robot wave (for cello and bass): The ball-and-socket joint of the left arm must be free of tension so that low strings can vibrate. Have students practice waving their left arm like a robot.[5]

3. Manual assist: Cellists and bassists may benefit from partner activities or by placing their elbow against the wall as they practice the shoulder swivel (see Video 13.16).

4. Pivot: The second finger of the left hand touches the collarbone; then the arm rotates while the elbow remains relatively still.[6] See Video 13.17.

COMBINED VIBRATO ACTIVITIES

Once violinists, violists, cellists, and bassists can perform the previous exercises, the following activities can be completed as a group:

1. Polish the string: In third or fourth position, lightly touch the string and slide back and forth (the distance of a minor third), decrease the distance of the sliding motion, and increase the speed.
2. Simulate the bowing motion in the air while vibrating silently on the string.
3. Practice the vibrato motion with a metronome, using controlled rhythmic practice. Set the metronome to 60 beats per minute and perform pitch oscillations above and below the note: eighth notes (duple), eighth notes (triple), sixteenth notes, and septuplets.

NOTES

1. Rolland, P., Mutchler, M. & Hellebrandt, F. (2010). *The teaching of action in string playing.* (3rd ed.). Urbana, IL: Illinois String Research Associates.
2. Cowden, R. L. (1972). A comparison of first and third position approaches to violin instruction. *Journal of Research in Music Education, 20*(4), 505–509.
3. MacLeod, R. B. & Geringer, J. M. (2017). What's the frequency? *The Strad,* July, 50–55.
4. Hamann, D. L. & Gillespie, R. (2013). *Strategies for teaching strings: Building a successful string and orchestra program.* (3rd ed.). Oxford, New York: Oxford University Press.
5. Fiste, J. (2007). *Celloprofessor.com.* Retrieved from www.celloprofessor.com/Cello-Vibrato.html.
6. Allen, M., Gillespie, R. & Tellejohn Hayes, P. (2004). *Essential technique for strings 2000.* Milwaukee, WI: Hal Leonard Corporation.

Index

Note: Page numbers in *italics* indicate figures and in **bold** indicate tables on the corresponding pages.